D1566624

American Individualism
(1922)

and

The Challenge to Liberty
(1934)

Also published by the Hoover Presidential Library Association

The Problems of Lasting Peace Revisited
A Scholarly Conference (1986)
THOMAS T. THALKEN, ED.

Doors of Opportunity
The Life and Legacy of Herbert Hoover (1988)
FRANK T. NYE, JR.

Herbert Hoover and the Historians (1989)
ELLIS W. HAWLEY, PATRICK G. O'BRIEN,
PHILIP T. ROSEN, ALEXANDER DECONDE

American Individualism

The Challenge to Liberty

Herbert Hoover

Herbert Hoover Presidential Library Association, Inc.
West Branch, Iowa

Library of Congress Cataloging in Publication Data

Hoover, Herbert, 1874-1964.
  [American individualism]
  American individualism : and, the challenge to liberty / by Herbert Hoover
    219 p   cm.
    ISBN 0-938469-04-5 : $19.95. -- ISBN 0-938469-05-3 (pbk.) : $11.95
1. Individualism.   2. United States--Social conditions--1 918-1932.   3. Liberalism--United States--History.   4. Liberty.   5. Collectivism.
6. United States--Constitutional history.   7. United States--Economic policy--1933-1945.   I. Hoover, Herbert, 1874-1964.   Challenge to liberty.   1989.   II. Title.
HM136.H6 1989
338.973'009042--dc20   89-2158
                                                           CIP

Herbert Hoover Presidential Library Association, Inc.
P.O. Box 696
West Branch, Iowa 52358

Manufactured in the United States of America.

Preface

In his long, productive life, Herbert Hoover played many parts. While his various careers as mining engineer, relief organizer, Cabinet officer, president and elder statesman have attracted renewed interest in recent years, none has more relevance to our own time than Hoover's role as a philosopher of modern conservative thought. In the dim light of the 1920s, following his successful campaigns to feed Belgium and a dozen other countries, his service as Woodrow Wilson's food czar and his selection to be Secretary of Commerce in the Harding administration, Hoover distilled his experience and fashioned a creed.

"There is somewhere to be found a plan of individualism and associational activities," he wrote, "that will preserve the initiative, the inventiveness, the individuality, the character of men and yet will enable us to synchronize socially and economically this gigantic machine that we have built out of applied science."

Hoover's message in *American Individualism* was not so gray as his prose. Like most one-time Progressives, he looked forward to perpetual advance, spurred on by technology, inhibited only by irrational politicians, greedy interest groups, and what he called "individualism run riot." His was an incremental idealism, wherein personal success was tempered and purified by service to others. "Character is made in the community as well as in the individual by assuming responsibilities," wrote the man who had abandoned his engineering career to feed war-ravaged Europe, "not by escape from them."

In his 1922 work, the future president envisioned a delicate balancing act between capitalists, workers and a public represented by the national government. Should one group gain authority over the others, the result would be fascism, socialism, or tyranny by bureaucracy. And individualism—the mainspring of American greatness—would be crippled for good.

"We might as well talk of abolishing individualism as a basis of successful society." Individual minds nurtured the seeds of social progress. "Its stimulus is competition. Its safeguard is education Its greatest mentor is free speech and voluntary organization for the public good." Washington had a critical function in guaranteeing equality of opportunity, for Hoover an essential condition if Americans were to adopt his new brand of individualism—generous enough to promote social justice, self-confident enough to ward off government's deadening hand, rigorous enough to prevent any interest group from gaining dominance.

It wasn't difficult to trace the origin of Hoover's faith. Out of his own Quaker background came an insistence on the divine spark within each man and woman. His personal struggle for professional recognition led to an unshakeable belief in "the emery board of competition." For Hoover, the ideal of co-operative association, first tested in Belgium, later honed through the Food Administration and now applied in his own land at thousands of Red Cross units, Community Chests, YMCAs and settlement houses, held the heartbeat of what he called the American System—a form of self-government outside of political government, and a fragile inheritance elected officials were sworn to protect by constantly watering the grassroots of opportunity in what Hoover labeled the Individualism State.

Twelve years would pass before Hoover's next attempt at codifying values. *The Challenge to Liberty* was necessarily a very different work, less a summons to cooperation than a warning against incipient fascism. "I am no more fond of the Wall Street model of liberty than I am of the Pennsylvania Avenue model," asserted the former president, for whom the Bill of Rights took precedence over property rights. Now, as in 1922, Hoover wrote in the shadow of revolution, nationalistic frenzy and economic confusion. But he did not fear Depression-era mobs in the streets of American cities. The threat to liberty was more subtle than that.

What Hoover termed "the tragedy of Liberty" followed a similar pattern on both sides of the Atlantic: "idealism without realism, slogans, phrases and statements destructive to confidence in existing institutions, demands for violent action against slowly curable ills; unfair representation that sporadic wickedness in the system itself." Next came the man on horseback, demanding delegation of authority from elected representatives, denouncing all opposition and exploiting propagandists in the pay of the state.

"Liberty dies of the water from her own well—free speech—poisoned by untruth," wrote Hoover. Again he paid tribute to his American System, with its enthronement of the individual and its insistence on social conscience as the price for personal achievement. Competition must co-exist with cooperation. America must reject monopoly and stratification alike. He assailed debased currency, limits on production, a government competing with private enterprise, quotas, and regimentation. Above all, he warned of "three implacable spirits" that animate all bureaucracies, "self-perpetuation, expansion, and an incessant demand for more power."

Critics responded by painting Hoover as a man with a theory. Having raised him to office, it then shackled his imagination and paved the way for ultimate defeat.

According to this school of thought, the former president was a victim of his own certainties.

Yet Hoover wrote out of a genuine anxiety for the future of liberty—and of the classical liberalism that produced both freedom and abundance. He concluded his appeal with words that retain their fire, more than half a century after they were written. The structure of human betterment, said Hoover, "cannot be built upon foundations of materialism or business, but upon the bedrock of individual character in free men and women. It must be built by those who, holding to ideals of high purpose, using the molds of justice, lay brick upon brick from the materials of scientific research, the painstaking sifting of truth from collections of fact and experience, the advancing ideas, morals and spiritual inspirations. Any other foundations are sand, any other mold is distorted; and any other bricks are without straw."

The Herbert Hoover Presidential Library Association is pleased to make available this special edition of *American Individualism* and *The Challenge to Liberty* in the conviction that both remain in their provocative way as timely in thought as they are timeless in expression.

Richard Norton Smith
Director
Hoover Presidential Library-Museum
West Branch, Iowa

Contents

Editor's Note

American Individualism was first published by Doubleday, Page and Company in Garden City, New York, in 1922. It was reissued in 1923, 1928, and 1934. The Herbert Hoover Presidential Library Association issued the work as a pamphlet in the mid-1970s. A Russian translation, Американски Индивидуапизмь, was first published in Sofia by Godina in February 1924. A Polish translation, *Indywidualizm Amerykański*, was published in Detroit by K.E. Szymański in 1930.

Charles Scribner's Sons published the first edition of *The Challenge to Liberty* in 1934 and reprinted it twice in 1935, bringing the total number of copies published to over 110,000. All subsequent major reprints have been copies of the Scribner's impression. The text of the present work is based on the first editions, now reset with with inconsistencies in spelling and capitalization corrected. This is the first time that *American Individualism* and *The Challenge to Liberty* have appeared in the same volume.

Mark M. Dodge
Claremont, California

Introduction

George H. Nash

On September 13, 1919 Herbert Hoover returned to the United States a troubled man. Ten months before, at the conclusion of the First World War, he had gone to Europe at President Woodrow Wilson's request to administer relief to a continent veering toward catastrophe. Across vast stretches of Europe, as 1919 began, famine, disease, and bloody revolution threatened to sunder a civilization already deeply wounded by "the war to end war." While Wilson and the Allied leaders struggled to draft a peace treaty at Versailles, Hoover and his American Relief Administration delivered food to literally millions of people, reorganized the transportation and communications networks of nations prostrate from conflict, and helped to check the advance of Bolshevik revolution surging from the East. Thanks in considerable measure to the Herculean efforts of Hoover and his staff, perhaps one-third of the population of postwar Europe was saved from starvation and death.

As Hoover journeyed back to America, his personal reputation was at its zenith. From Finland to Armenia, from the streets of Vienna to the plains of eastern Poland, his name—and that of the American Relief Administration—were acclaimed. In America he was called "the Napoleon of Mercy." In the words of John Maynard Keynes, he was "the only man who emerged from the ordeal of Paris with an enhanced reputation."[1]

Yet Hoover, that autumn, was not content. For several months he had pleaded with the Allied leaders at Versailles to lift their blockade of the defeated German enemy and allow the healing currents of peaceful exchange to flow. Only after a long, wearisome struggle did he attain this objective. Every day at the peace conference he had witnessed a dispiriting display of national rivalry, greed, myopia, and vengefulness. He had seen, too, the sometimes violent attempts of reformers and radicals to construct a new social order on the principles of Marxist socialism. It was a time, he observed, of "stupendous social ferment and revolution."[2]

Hoover returned to his native land (he soon told friends) with "two convictions...dominant in my mind." The first was that the ideology of socialism, as tested before him in Europe, was a catastrophic failure. Socialism's fundamental premises, said Hoover, were false—the premises that the "impulse of altruism" could alone maintain productivity and that bureaucracy at the top could determine the most productive roles for each individual. Only the "primary school of competition," Hoover countered, could do that. Oblivious to this truth and to the fundamental human impulse of self-interest, socialism had "wrecked itself on the rock of production." It was unable to motivate men and women to produce sufficient goods for the needs of society. And without increased productivity and resultant plenty, neither social harmony nor an improved standard of living for the

[1]John Maynard Keynes, *The Economic Consequences of the Peace* (New York, 1920), 274n.

[2]Herbert Hoover, "The Safety of New-born Democracies," *Forum* 62 (December 1919), 551.

masses would occur. To Hoover the economic demoralization of Europe in 1919, with its attendant shortages and suffering, were the direct result of the bankruptcy of socialism.[3]

Hoover's second conviction was also firmly held. More than ever before he sensed the "enormous distance" that America had drifted from Europe during the one-hundred fifty years of nationhood.[4] To Hoover it now seemed that "irreconcilable conflicts" in ideals and experience separated the Old World from the New.[5] The New World, he came to believe, was remote from the imperialism, fanatic ideologies, "age-old hates," racial antipathies, dictatorships, power politics, and class stratifications of Europe. What he had witnessed at the Versailles peace conference, he came to believe, was something far more profound than "the intrigues of diplomacy or the foibles of European statesmen." It was "the collision of civilizations that had grown three hundred years apart."[6]

These sentiments of Hoover's to some extent antedated the trauma of 1919. Before the outbreak of the Great War, Hoover had been an extraordinary successful international mining engineer. Born in Iowa in 1874, by the time he was forty years old he had spent most of his adulthood outside the United States—in environments as various as the goldfields of the Australian outback, the coal mines of northern China, the rain forests of Burma, and the boardrooms of London.

[3]Ibid., 551, 560-561.

[4]Ibid., 551.

[5]Herbert Hoover, *The Memoirs of Herbert Hoover,* Volume 1: *Years of Adventure* (New York, 1951), 473.

[6]Ibid., 479.

This early and prolonged exposure to foreign civilizations led Hoover to reflect on the remarkable contrasts in politics, economics, and philosophy of life between other societies and his own. Why, he wondered, was America so different? Why was America unique?

That America *was* different Hoover was certain. "Every homecoming" to his native shores, he later wrote, "was an inspiration." In America he found

> a greater kindness, a greater neighborliness, a greater sense of individual responsibility, a lesser poverty, a greater comfort and security of our people, a wider spread of education, a wider diffusion of the finer arts and appreciation of them, a greater freedom of spirit, a wider opportunity for our children, and higher hopes of the future, than in any other country in the world.[7]

This is how Hoover felt after his numerous engineering journeys before 1914. It was how he felt in September 1919 as he headed home.

Yet Hoover was by no means complacent. During 1919 the United States itself experienced bitter and frightening upheavals: a massive strike in the steel industry, a police strike and mob violence in Boston, a general strike in Seattle, race riots in twenty towns and cities, the lynching of seventy-eight blacks, the founding of the Communist Party, and the attempted assassination-by-bombing of several public officials. Coming back to America from Europe, Hoover sensed that his country was vulnerable to the afflictions he had witnessed abroad. To an assembly of mining engineers he declared early in 1920:

> We face a Europe still at war; still amid social revolutions; some of its peoples still slacking on production, millions starving; and therefore the safety of its civilization is still

[7]Herbert Hoover, *The Challenge to Liberty* (New York, 1934), 38.

hanging by a slender thread. Every wind that blows carries to
our shores an infection of social disease from this great
ferment; every convulsion there has an economic reaction upon
our own people.[8]

Hoover implored his fellow citizens not to turn their country
into "a laboratory for experiment in foreign social diseases."[9]
Instead, he said, "A definite American substitute is needed for
these disintegrating theories of Europe"—a substitute
grounded in "our national Instincts" and "the normal
development of our national institutions."[10]

In numerous speeches and articles in 1919-1920 Hoover
began to define this American "substitute." The foundation
of the distinctive American social philosophy, he asserted,
was the principle of equality of opportunity: the idea that no
one should be "handicapped in securing that particular niche
in the community to which his abilities and character entitle
him." Unlike Europe, where oppressive class barriers had
generated misery and discontent, the American social system
was based upon "negation of class." A society, said Hoover,
in which there is "a constant flux of individuals in the
community, upon the basis of ability and character, is a
moving virile mass...."[11] Such a society was America.

This did not mean that Hoover was a nativist or
standpatter. Time and time again in these turbulent months he
emphatically made clear that American ideals as he
understood them comported with neither radicalism nor

[8]Herbert Hoover, inaugural address to the American Institute of
Mining and Metallurgical Engineers (A.I.M.M.E.), February 17,
1920, Public Statements File, Herbert Hoover Presidential Library,
West Branch Iowa.

[9]Hoover, "Safety of New-born Democracies," 561.

[10]Ibid.

[11]Hoover, inaugural address to the A.I.M.M.E., February 17, 1920.

reaction. To Hoover the convulsions gripping Europe were an understandable response to long-festering social injustice. To be sure, the socialist panacea was a ghastly error, but for Hoover the alternative was not the *status quo ante bellum.* "We shall never remedy justifiable discontent," he said, "until we eradicate the misery which the ruthlessness of individualism has imposed upon a minority."[12] According to Hoover the solution of the problems of productivity and "better division of the products of industry" lay not with the extremists but with "the liberal world of moderate men, working upon the safe foundation of experience."[13]

And this, in 1920, was where Hoover perceived himself to be. A Bull Moose supporter of Theodore Roosevelt in 1912, a member of Woodrow Wilson's war cabinet during the recent conflict, a self-styled "independent Progressive" as 1920 began, Hoover formally identified with the Republican party early in the year and unsuccessfully stood for its presidential nomination. A few months later, President-elect Warren Harding appointed Hoover as his Secretary of Commerce.

On March 4, 1921 Hoover entered Harding's Cabinet and plunged with vigor into the gigantic task of reconstruction from the most terrible war the world had ever known. In short order Hoover became one of the three or four most influential men in American public life. It was said of him that he was the Secretary of Commerce and the undersecretary of every other department. But even as he applied his extraordinary energies to a formidable array of practical problems, the old questions continued to haunt him:

[12]Hoover, "Safety of New-born Democracies," 562.
[13]Ibid., 561.

How could America avoid the follies of Europe? How could
the American system be strengthened in an age of revolution?
Why was America so different? Why was America unique?

In late 1921 Hoover decided to distill from his unique
experiences a coherent understanding of the American
experiment he cherished. The result was to be the book
American Individualism. The genesis of Hoover's work was
an undelivered convocation address at an American university
that autumn. Encouraged by his friend the journalist Mark
Sullivan, Hoover decided to publish his manuscript; in the
spring of 1922 it appeared as an article in the magazine
World's Work.[14] Late in the year, in a somewhat revised
form, *American Individualism* was published as a book.

Hoover's volume represented the crystallization of the
attitudes and perceptions mentioned earlier in this essay.
According to Hoover, the revolutionary upheavals of World
War I and its aftermath had produced a world in ferment. In
this cauldron several ideologies (he called them "social
philosophies") were competing for the minds of men, among
them Communism, Socialism, Syndicalism, and Capitalism.
To Hoover, who had seen the vicious results that emanate
from a blending of "bestial instincts" with idealistic
humanitarian jargon, the need for a definition of the
"American Individualism."

By this term he definitely did not mean unfettered, old-
fashioned laissez-faire, as he expectedly emphasized in the

[14]Mark Sullivan to Hoover, October 13, 1921, "*American
Individualism*, 1921-1922," Commerce Papers; Herbert Hoover
Papers, Herbert Hoover Presidential Library; Hoover, "American
Individualism," *World's Work* 43 (April 1922), 584-588. The
caption under the title of Hoover's magazine article was revealing:
"The Genius of Our Government and of Our Industry Reaffirmed
Against Old World Philosophies and Experiments."

book. Hoover was anxious that individual initiative always be stimulated and rewarded; initiative, in fact, was one of the character traits he most admired. Progress, he declared, "is almost solely dependent" on the few "creative minds" who "create or who carry discoveries to widespread application." But *too much* individualism—"individualism run riot"— could lead to injustice and even tyranny in the form of domination of government and business by the powerful. The "values of individualism," therefore, said Hoover, must be "tempered"—tempered as they indeed had been in American history—by "that firm and fixed ideal of American individualism—*an equality of opportunity.*" Equality of opportunity, "the demand for a fair chance as the basis of American life"—this, in Hoover's words, was "our precious social ideal." Hoover insisted that equal opportunity and a "fair chance" for individuals to develop their abilities were "the sole source of progress" and the fundamental impulse behind American civilization for three centuries.

Hoover did not believe that equality of opportunity was automatically self-sustaining in a modern, technological economy. A certain measure of governmental regulation and legislation {such as anti-trust laws and inheritance taxes on large fortunes) was necessary, he felt, to prevent economic autocracy, *in*equality of opportunity, and the throttling of individual initiative. To Hoover it was imperative that "*we keep the social solution free from frozen strata of classes.*" The "human particles" (as he later put it) must be able to "move freely in the social solution." Some governmental regulation was necessary to this end.

Hoover, then, was no Social Darwinist. In his book he explicitly repudiated laissez-faire, which he defined as "every man for himself and the devil take the hindmost." It was, he stated, an outmoded social doctrine which America had abandoned "when we adopted the ideal of equality—the fair chance of Abraham Lincoln." At the same time, Hoover unequivocally rejected socialism and the all-intrusive state. In effect the Secretary of Commerce was counselling a careful course of reform without revolution, avoiding the "equal dangers" of radicalism and reaction. Citing growing evidence of industrial *self*-regulation such as burgeoning trade associations and cooperatives, Hoover believed that a new era in American life was dawning: an era blending self-interest with the ethic of service and cooperation. In short, American individualism—"the most precious possession of American civilization"—was the still-valid formula for national progress.

Hoover's little book was no idle excursion into the realm of political philosophy. The publication of *American Individualism* in December 1922, in fact, had an immediate and pressing purpose. During the preceding months the United States had been riven by its most important industrial strife since the 1890s. In April more than half a million coal miners went out on a nationwide strike. Less than three months later 400,000 railroad workers joined them. As the two tremendous strikes dragged on through the summer, the nation's supply of coal for the coming winter plummeted and her transportation facilities headed for total breakdown. In the words of the Secretary of Labor, America appeared to be "on the verge of industrial collapse."

Although the strikes were finally resolved by early autumn (Hoover was intimately involved in the episode), many Americans were apprehensive. Social dislocation of alarming propositions had again manifested itself. In the Congressional elections that autumn the Republican party lost

70 seats in the House of Representatives; in the economically hard-pressed states of the American heartland radical agrarians made notable gains. Was a new storm of divisiveness and demagoguery brewing?

Herbert Hoover appeared to fear that it was. Sometime in 1922 he evidently decided to convert his article on "American Individualism" into a book as an antidote to the rising tide of unrest. Although the precise date of his decision is uncertain, it was probably no accident that within two days of the November election Hoover's staff took steps to rush his book into print at once. In an office memorandum on November 9 Hoover's assistant George Barr Baker explained the need for haste: immediate publication, he said, would "secure immediate dissemination of the ideas it contains" and leave Hoover "free to expand certain related ideas" in the spring. "With the public mind in its present state," Baker added, "and with the certainty that the next Congress will be very largely controlled by men with extreme views, of both parties, we recognize that the service this book can render must be immediate."[15] Another Hoover associate, Edgar Rickard, agreed. Appealing to no fewer than sixty friends to help in the book's distribution, Rickard declared that *American Individualism* was "particularly needed" in "this time of unrest."[16] Rickard believed that Hoover's book would "do much toward quieting the minds of people who are disturbed by present economic conditions."[17]

[15]George Barr Baker, memorandum, November 9, 1922, "*American Individualism*, 1922-1923 and Undated (5)," Commerce Papers.

[16]Edgar Rickard, text of letter to his friends, n.d., ibid.

[17]Edgar Rickard to Arthur Ryerson, December 20, 1922, "*American Individualism*, 1922-1923 and Undated (4)," Commerce Papers. See also Rickard to Howard J. Heinz, December 2, 1922, ibid.

Throughout the rest of November, Hoover's assistants labored to expedite the publishing process and lubricate the levers of publicity. On December 11, 1922, only five weeks after the election, *American Individualism* was published by Doubleday, Page, & Co. With energy and thoroughness Hoover's publisher and friends circulated his "sermon" (as Rickard called it) throughout the land.[18] Every newly-elected Congressman from the Middle West, for instance, received a free copy, as did professors of economics in various colleges.[19] Through Hoover's extensive network of associates in his wartime and postwar humanitarian work approximately 2,000 copies were distributed. By late January 1923, less than two months after publication, more than 9,600 copies had been sold outright and another 4,600 were on sale in book stores. The book was already in its third printing.[20]

With the exception of the socialist press and the *New Republic*, the reception of reviewers to Hoover's book was generally friendly.[21] The *New York Times Book Review* predicted that in content, if not style, *American Individualism* would rank "among the few great formulations of American political theory."[22] In Europe as well as in America,

---

[18]Rickard to Heinz, December 2, 1922; various correspondence, 1922-1923, passim, in the *American Individualism* files, Commerce Papers.

[19]Arthur W. Page to Frank C. Page, January 24, 1923, "*American Individualism*, 1922-1923 and Undated (3)," Commerce Papers.

[20]Ibid.; Rickard to J.F. Lucey, January 16, 1923, "*American Individualism*, 1922-1923 and Undated (4)," Commerce Papers.

[21]See the two summaries of comment compiled by a member of Hoover's staff, February 9 and 21, 1923, "*American Individualism*, 1922-1923 and Undated ," Commerce Papers.

[22]*New York Times Book Review*, December 17, 1922, 1.

Hoover's book found interested readers; it was eventually translated into German, Polish, Japanese, and Bulgarian.

Hoover's apotheosis of the United States as a land dedicated to the ideal of equal opportunity evoked particular enthusiasm from the distinguished historian Frederick Jackson Turner, exponent of the "frontier thesis." Hoover's "meaty little book," said Turner, "contains the New and the Old Testament of the American gospel and I wish it a wide circulation."[23] Perhaps it is not coincidental that when Turner's book *The Frontier in American History* was published in 1920, he had given a copy to Hoover, who read it (according to his secretary) "with very great interest."[24]

With the rise of "Coolidge prosperity" in the mid-1920s, the labor conflicts and social traumas of 1921-1922 receded. Whatever *American Individualism*'s contribution to this process may have been, Hoover's little "sermon" helped to establish him as one of the principal spokesmen for what came to be called the New Era. By 1928 Hoover was a candidate for the presidency. Looking back that year on the book he had published a half-decade before, Hoover told an acquaintance, "I am afraid the book is a little out of date as it was written when we were somewhat more exercised over socialistic and communistic movements than we need to be today."[25]

He could not foresee that his philosophy of American individualism was about to face its starkist challenge.

***

[23]Frederick Jackson Turner to Richard S. Emmet (a Hoover secretary), January 18, 1923, Commerce Papers.

[24]Emmet to Turner, January 27, 1923, ibid.

[25]Hoover to Homer Guck, May 8, 1928, "*American Individualism, 1922-1923 and Undated,*" ibid.

What a difference a half-decade can make. In early 1928 Herbert Hoover was nearing the pinnacle of a spectacular public career. Five years later he was an ex-president, defeated overwhelmingly at the polls, his achievements and social philosophy seemingly repudiated forever by his own people.

Throughout the long months of 1933 and early 1934 Hoover maintained public silence as the New Deal of President Franklin Delano Roosevelt unfolded. Hoover adopted this posture for several reasons. He did not wish, by any partisan act, to jeopardize, or appear to jeopardize, economic recovery during the national emergency. He doubted that any comments of his would do much good in the current public atmosphere, poisoned as he considered it to be by the incessant "smearing" of his record by the opposition. He hoped also that as New Deal measures failed (which he expected them to do) the American people would learn from disillusioning experience and return to their traditional values.

But if Hoover stayed aloof from the fray for tactical reasons, he was far from indifferent to what he was. At the climax of the election campaign of 1932, he had portrayed the decision facing the American electorate as more than a choice between two men and two parties. It was a "contest between two philosophies of government," an election that would determine the nation's course for "over a century to come."[26] Everything that had happened since had reinforced this conviction. Hoover thought that the New Deal was no simple spate of reform nor pragmatic response to economic distress; it was nothing less than a form of collectivism that would

[26]Hoover, in a speech in New York City, October 31, 1932; complete text in *Public Papers of the Presidents of the United States: Herbert Hoover...1932-33* (Washington, DC, 1977), 656-679.

"destroy the very foundations of the American system of life."[27] In September 1933 he told a close friend:

> The impending battle in this country obviously will be between a properly regulated individualism (which I have always expounded as "American Individualism") and sheer socialism. That, directly or indirectly, is likely to be the great political battle for some years to come.[28]

Although Hoover continued to use the term "American Individualism" (and even considered reissuing his book of that title in 1933),[29] increasingly he invoked another word to describe his—and America's social philosophy. That word was liberalism. Liberalism, said Hoover late in 1933,

> is an intangible, imponderable thing. It is the freedom of men's minds and spirits. It was born with the Renaissance, was re-enforced with the Reformation, was brought to reality by the American revolution, and has survived by much suffering down to the corruption of the great war [World War I]. Today we are engaged in creating regimented men, not free men, both in spirit and in economic life.[30]

Hoover contended that the progress of American civilization had come from "its fidelity to true liberalism." To be sure, our liberal economic system had "often bred autocracies and privilege which in themselves tended to stifle freedom." But, said Hoover, until March 4, 1933 (the day of President Roosevelt's inauguration) America had "kept the lamp of liberalism alight by reform and not by revolution."[31]

[27]Ibid., 657.

[28]Hoover to Edward Eyre Hunt, September 14, 1933, Post-Presidential Individual file, Hoover Papers.

[29]Ibid.

[30]Hoover to Will Irwin, December 16, 1933, ibid..

[31]Ibid.

For Hoover the fundamentals of historic liberation were embodied in the United States Constitution, above all in the Bill of Rights. Increasingly in 1933-1934, the Bill of Rights—that charter (in his words) of "ordered individual liberty"—was on his mind. "The discouraging thing," he lamented privately, "is that for some fancied economic boom the American people are prepared to sacrifice their most fundamental possession."[32] Events in Europe, where Hitler and Mussolini were on the march, added a somber dimension to his concerns. The manifestations of recrudescent statism were worldwide. By the end of 1933, as vast New Deal programs like the NRA proliferated, the ex-president believed that the policies of the Roosevelt administration were "driving more clearly to Fascism and Nazism than even toward socialism."[33]

By early 1934 Hoover was at work on a manuscript that would confront the ascendant statist ideologies on the terrain where he felt they must be fought: the terrain of philosophy and principle. Hoover solicited the comments of a number of old friends, notably the advertising executive Bruce Barton and the editor of *Woman's Home Companion*, Gertrude Lane.[34] Hoover was not interested in making money on his forthcoming book; he told a friend that what did matter was the conveyance of his message to the public in his own manner and idiom.[35] He turned down a chance to publish two articles based on the book in *American Magazine* for

[32]Hoover to Henry J. Allen, November 14, 1933, ibid.

[33]Hoover to Irwin, December 16, 1933.

[34]See correspondence with Barton and Lane, 1934, Post-Presidential Individual file, Hoover Papers; also Edgar Rickard diary, June 19 and 21, 1934, Herbert Hoover Presidential Library.

[35]Rickard diary, July 14, 1934.

$25,000, preferring instead to publish them in the *Saturday
Evening Post* for $10,000.[36] Nor was Hoover interested (he
said) in the book's possible political reverberations. It was
not intended for the 1934 Congressional election campaign,
he asserted in June, "as I have no interest in its party effect.
The Old Guard are not likely to approve it any more than will
the Republican Progressives."[37]

For a time Hoover was apparently uncertain whether to
publish his book before the election at all. At least one of his
intimate friends, Lewis Strauss, advised him to wait.[38] But
by early summer Hoover had determined to bring his work
out in September—the very start of the Fall campaign.[39]
"The time is getting short if this book is to be of service," he
told Barton on June 23.[40] He later informed a friend that if
he had held off until after the election, Republicans could
legitimately have accused him of "shirking my
responsibility." "In any event," he added, "the campaign
itself may enliven a discussion of the question, and that we
have to have."[41]

Throughout the summer Hoover prepared to unleash his
salvo with as much effect as possible. He arranged for the
Saturday Evening Post to print two excerpts just prior to
publication. He considered a plan to distribute 25,000 copies

[36]Ibid.

[37]Hoover to Bruce Barton, June 7, 1934, Bruce Barton Papers, State
Historical Society of Wisconsin.

[38]Arch W. Shaw to Hoover, August 8, 1934, Post-Presidential
Individual file, Hoover Papers.

[39]Hover to Gertrude Lane, July 3, 1934, ibid.

[40]Hoover to Barton, June 23, 1934, Barton Papers.

[41]Hoover to Henry J. Allen, September 17, 1934, Post-Presidential
Individual file, Hoover Papers.

of his book to political workers (presumably Republicans).[42] He conceived the idea of asking "friendly college professors" to prepare a manifesto defending his book against "the deluge of mud which may be coming." After all, he recalled, 1,300 professors had publicly petitioned him not to sign the Smoot-Hawley tariff bill in 1930. "I do not see why they should not make a declaration on Liberty itself apropos of this book."[43]

The prospects for wide circulation of Hoover's opus were enhanced during the summer when the Book-of-the-Month Club adopted it for October distribution. But to Hoover's annoyance the Club decided to offer it conjointly with a defense of the New Deal written by Secretary of Agriculture Henry Wallace: a book entitled *New Frontiers*. To Hoover the Club "would never have dreamed of buying [Wallace's book] if it had not been from a desire to appear to be so terribly unbiased."

> I am perhaps over-suspicious these days, but when an old and reliable newspaper friend informs me this morning that he has just had an offer of $2,000 from quarters which unquestionably represent the opposition if he would secretely [sic] get copies of the text, and when my mail is tampered with,...I begin to think that this is no longer a Republic.[44]

As the moment of publication approached, Hoover's excitement intensified. He hoped that the publisher, Charles Scribner's Sons, would keep an advance copy out of the hands of New Dealers, "as they have no scruples as to the methods which they use."[45] On August 10, his sixtieth

[42]Edgar Rickard diary, August 3,6, and 22, 1934.

[43]Hoover to Arch W. Shaw, August 22, 1934; copy in Barton Papers.

[44]Hoover to Barton, August 12 and 22, 1934, Barton Papers.

[45]Hoover to Barton, July 31, 1934, Barton Papers.

birthday, Hoover disclosed to a Republican senator that he would soon "bust loose into print." "I hope that it will do some good," he added. "At least it will relieve my pent up feelings."[46] A few days later he told another friend that his "conscience would not stand further suppression despite much contrary advice from friends."[47]

At times that summer Hoover seemed almost despairing. On July 9 he told Gertrude Lane that his book was "my last shot at public service:"

> I do not over-estimate the book's usefulness; but it clears my own conscience and does what I can for people groping in the dark. Privately, I have no expectation that a nation which has once cut loose from its moorings to definite human rights and places them at the disposal of the State will ever return to them. History does not move that way, and those who sling to such a philosophy are just part of the wreckage. We can nevertheless yell "help, help."[48]

At other times he seemed more hopeful. On August 12 he informed Barton that in the past month the country had "turned definitely against the New Deal."[49] To Hoover this development made the need for his book even more compelling. For when the revulsion against the New Deal comes, he wrote in September, "we will have laid such foundations that will make the revulsion to the right instead of to the left. That, in fact, is one of the major objectives of the book."[50]

[46]Hoover to Warren Austin, August 10, 1934, Post-Presidential Individual file, Hoover Papers.

[47]Hoover to George Akerson, August 14, 1934, ibid.

[48]Hoover to Gertrude Lane, July 9, 1934, ibid.

[49]Hoover to Barton, August 12, 1934, Barton Papers.

[50]Hoover to Henry J. Allen, September 17, 1934.

If Hoover's mood seemed at times nearly apocalyptic, it no doubt reflected the incredible ordeal he had been through. Striving conscientiously throughout his presidency against the greatest economic calamity in American history, he had found himself relentlessly caricatured as a cold and heartless leader. Shanty-towns had been derisively named "Hoovervilles;" across the land millions had seemed to hold him almost personally responsible for the loss of their homes, their farms, their jobs. Rejection at the polls in 1932 had not brought catharsis but instead the collapse of the nation's banks during the last days of his presidency—a debacle deliberately precipitated, he contended, by President-elect Roosevelt's refusal to cooperate with the outgoing administration. Nor had the advent of the New Deal brought surcease and reconciliation. As recently as February 1934, Roosevelt's Secretary of the Interior, Harold Ickes, had publicly derided Hoover as "the champion of that ruthless exploiting individualism that was in the main responsible for the terrible economic situation in which we found ourselves."[51] No wonder his regimen of silence was difficult to bear.

As Hoover prepared to reenter public debate in the fall of 1934, he seemed especially anxious to counter an expected "deluge of defamation" that his book was the creed of a reactionary. He, therefore, asked the nationally respected liberal Republican editor, William Allen White, to issue a laudatory review to the press on the day of publication. In this way Hoover hoped to neutralize some of the negative stereotyping sure to ensue.[52]

[51]*New York Times* February 9, 1934, 1.

[52]Hoover to Barton, July 20, 30, August 22, 1934, Barton Papers.

On September 28, 1934, Hoover's *cri de coer* at last appeared. Although he had originally entitled his manuscript *American Liberalism*,[53] the book as published bore the more militant title *The Challenge to Liberty*. According to Hoover, the American system of liberty, a system infused by the philosophy of historic liberalism, was under fundamental assault. Where liberalism championed the individual as master of the state and possessor of inalienable rights, alternative philosophies were now boldly advocating "the idea of the servitude of the individual to the state." Among these philosophies—all sharing this fundamental premise—were Socialism, Communism, Fascism, and National Regimentation (Hoover's term for the New Deal).

Hoover freely admitted that the American regime of liberty had at times been abused. Repeatedly in his book he expatiated on the need for reform and emphasized that America's traditional social philosophy was not one of unfettered laissez-faire. But Hoover insisted that the flaws in the American system were "marginal," corrigible, and far less pernicious than the "bureaucratic tyranny" that would inevitably accompany the collectivist alternatives. In a powerful conclusion Hoover drew the line:

> We cannot extend the mastery of government over the daily life of a people without somewhere making it master of the people's souls and thoughts. That is going on today. It is part of all regimentation.

> Even if the government conduct of business could give us the maximum of efficiency instead of least efficiency, it would be purchased at the cost of freedom. It would increase rather than decrease abuse and corruption, stifle initiative and invention, undermine the development of leadership, cripple the mental and spiritual energies of our people, extinguish equality of

[53]Shaw to Hoover, August 8, 1934.

opportunity, and dry up the spirit of liberty and the forces which make progress.

It is a false Liberalism that interprets itself into government dictation, or operation of commerce, industry and agriculture. Every move in that direction poisons the very springs of true Liberalism. It poisons political equality, free thought, free press, and equality of opportunity. It is the road not to liberty, but to less liberty. True Liberalism is found not in the striving to spread bureaucracy, but in striving to set bounds to it. Liberalism is a force proceeding from the deep realization that economic freedom cannot be sacrificed if political freedom is to be preserved.

The Challenge to Liberty was Hoover's first major public statement after he left the White House, and as he had anticipated, it was an "event." By early October *Challenge* was the best-selling non-fiction book in New York City and was on the best-seller list in nine of the principal book markets of the country.[54] By March 1935, six months after its publication, over 100,000 copies had been distributed, including 29,600 through the "trade" and 31,000 through the Book-of-the-Month Club.[55] In the grim Depression year of 1934 this was a creditable showing indeed.

Hoover and his allies labored assiduously to distribute the book far and wide. Nearly 11,000 copies were sent to libraries throughout the United States, 2,500 to editorialists, and 8,500 to an anti-New Deal organization known as the Crusaders. Seven hundred were shipped to selected preachers. Hoover personally took 13,000 copies which he then gave to Republican county chairmen, delegates to the 1932 Republican national convention, former associates in

[54]Barton to Hoover, October 11, 1934, Barton Papers.

[55]H. Meier, memorandum, March 22, 1935, "Books by HH: *The Challenge to Liberty*—Printing Arrangements," Post-Presidential Subject file, Hoover Papers.

his humanitarian relief organizations, and many more.[56] In all likelihood the cost of this immense effort was borne, directly or indirectly, by Hoover himself.

Reviewing *The Challenge to Liberty* and *New Frontiers* in the *Saturday Review of Literature*, the historian Allan Nevins described the two books as "opening guns in a great battle" that would "rage with increasing fury" until after the election of 1936.[57] In the weeks that followed, much of the response to Hoover's work bore a partisan cast. Unlike 1922, Hoover's new articulation of "American Liberalism" did not win general assent. To ardent New Dealers Hoover's book was dull, doctrinaire, and abstract.[58] The keynote of Hoover's book, said Professor Nevins, was "Caution," that of Wallace's book, "Vision."[59] Interior Secretary Ickes was more caustic. Hoover, he asserted, wanted "liberty of privilege:" "Mr. Hoover and those who think along with him don't seem to be concerned with the masses of the people who want decent living conditions and jobs with fair wages. They emphasize the right of those with property to be free from disturbance of any one."[60] Hoover must have wondered whether Ickes understood his argument.

Not all the response, by any means, was hostile. William Allen White, for instance, acclaimed *The Challenge to Liberty*

[56]See the various memoranda in the file cited in the preceding footnote.

[57]Allan Nevins, "The Battle of 1936 Begins," *Saturday Review of Literature* 11 (October 6, 1934), 15, 168, 170,172.

[58]See, for examples, the reviews in the *Christian Century*, *Commonweal*, *The Nation*, and the *Times Literary Supplement* in the autumn of 1934.

[59]Nevins, "Battle of 1936 Begins," 172.

[60]*New York Times*, September 5, 1934, 15.

as "an honest man's patriotic protest against shortcuts to economic security." According to White, Hoover was not an unyielding foe of the New Deal's objectives—only of its methods. The object of the New Deal, claimed White, was a "readjustment of our national income," guaranteeing both economic security to the "average man of no acquisitive talents" and a "chance to rise" to "the man with talents." According to White, Hoover also believed in "some fundamental reconstruction of the American economic system."

It is not known how Hoover reacted to White's assertion that he disagreed only with the New Deal's methods. But in his review White quoted from a letter that Hoover had recently written to him:

> I hope some day our people will learn that property rights are not the foundation of human liberty. Those foundations lie in the other rights which free the spirit of men—free conscience, worship, thought, opinion, expression, creativeness, security of home, family and justice...
>
> When governments take or destroy property rights they not only extinguish these motivations [toward enterprise and creativity] but they invariably use economic power to stifle the other rights, and they employ a lot of bureaucrats to rub it in. But unrestrained use of property rights by the individual can also abuse, dominate and extinguish the more precious liberties and securities. Therefore governments must enact laws against abuse and dominations and must umpire these matters. The activities of governments must be limited to that.

This, said Hoover, was the difference between "real liberalism" and its enemies.[61]

Perhaps the most dispassionate review of *The Challenge to Liberty* came from a long-time friend, Professor Wesley C.

[61]*New York Times*, September 28, 1934, 21.

Mitchell of Columbia University. "To call [Hoover] a reactionary or conservative," wrote Mitchell, "is as wrong as to call him a radical. He occupies a middle ground and wages a war on two fronts. Hence he is exposed more than most public men to misrepresentations."[62] Hoover was warmly grateful for Mitchell's comments.[63]

But as Hoover increasingly realized, the "middle ground" he tried to occupy was not holding. The political center of gravity was shifting, even if Hoover was not. He told William Allen White in 1937 that since the New Deal had "corrupted the label of liberalism for collectivism, coercion, [and] concentration of political power, it seem 'Historic Liberalism' must be conservativism by contrast."[64] The ex-president's political journey was completed. The Bull Mooser of 1912, the Wilsonian of World War I, the "independent progressive" of early 1920, the man whom Old Guard Republicans had tried in vain to block from the presidential nomination in 1928: he, Herbert Hoover, had become a man of the Right.

***

It is now sixty-seven years since *American Individualism* was published, and more than fifty since *The Challenge to Liberty* appeared. It is clear, in retrospect, that both books were in part *livres de circonstance*. Said Hoover of *The*

---

[62]Wesley C. Mitchell, "Mr. Hoover's 'The Challenge to Liberty,'" *Political Science Quarterly* 49 (December 1934); 599, (full review: 599-614).

[63]Hoover to Wesley C. Mitchell, December 17, 1934, Post-Presidential Individual file, Hoover Papers.

[64]Hoover to William Allen White, May 11, 1937, ibid.

Challenge to Liberty in mid-1934: "I have not written it for posterity. It is for service right now."[65]

And yet today, long after the circumstances that produced these books have disappeared, Hoover's creed continues to invite our attention. Few of our presidents have ventured self-consciously into the realm of political philosophy; Herbert Hoover did. Unlike most American men of affairs, who have been content to act on the public stage but not to meditate much about it, Hoover endeavored to define the nature of the American regime. This alone gives the books reprinted here an enduring interest.

The importance of these documents, however, transcends the scholarly concerns of historians and political scientists. For the books before us are not simply products of a receding past; to a considerable degree the ideological battles of Hoover's era are the battles of our own. And the interpretations we *make* of our past—particularly of the years 1921-1933—inevitably mold our perspectives on the crises of the present. To many individuals of the Left, for instance, the New Deal was essentially a moderate reform movement which saved American capitalism from destruction and averted a revolution. To Herbert Hoover, however, the New Deal *was* a revolution that wrought a profound transformation in the relationship of government to citizen, of government to economy—a transformation that would eventually, inevitably, enervate our liberties and the wellsprings of our property. Fifty years later the portents of the future are too

[65]Hoover to Barton, June 7, 1934

ambiguous to say with assurance that his prophecy was wrong.

Indeed, during the 1980s, the social philosophy expounded in *American Individualism* and *The Challenge to Liberty* has acquired an increasing resonance. For the first time in many years individuals in high office started to reexamine *in principle* social programs and assumptions that have dominated our politics for half a century. New themes have entered our public policy debates—themes like voluntarism, decentralization of government, restraint of bureaucracy, stimulation of private initiative and entrepreneurship, even reconsideration of the gold standard. New themes yet old themes: *Hooverian* themes.

There is a broader relevance still to the works reprinted in this volume. Of all the men who have been president of the United States, Herbert Hoover enjoyed more extensive acquaintance with foreign peoples and their social systems than any of his predecessors or successors. Hoover's perception of contrast between the Old World and the New was the experiential core of his social philosophy, and it gave him a fervent sense of American uniqueness. To him the United States was "one of the last few strongholds of human freedom."

Today, as in Hoover's time, that stronghold is under siege. Hoover called its values "American Individualism" and "Historic Liberalism;" for us, a more common term, perhaps, is "democratic capitalism." But whatever the label, the reality is clear: over much of the earth antipathetic social philosophies are regnant, and their spokesmen have little love for the philosophy of liberty.

In an era, then, when defenders of the American regime face daily assaults on our most precious values, the two books reprinted here have more than casual interest. Hoover knew that in this century of war and revolution it is philosophy, however perverted, that moves men for good or ill. It is imperative, therefore, that we comprehend our own. The two works republished here can contribute to our national self-understanding.

This is no academic exercise. From a lifetime of comparative social analysis Herbert Hoover derived this lesson: in the destinies of nations, ideas—and ideals—mattered.

They still do.

George H. Nash
West Branch, Iowa

American Individualism

INTRODUCTION

We have witnessed in this last eight years the spread of revolution over one-third of the world. The causes of these explosions lie at far greater depths than the failure of governments in war. The war itself in its last stages was a conflict of social philosophies—but beyond this the causes of social explosion lay in the great inequities and injustices of centuries flogged beyond endurance by the conflict and greed from restraint by the destruction of war. The urgent forces which drive human society have been plunged into a terrible furnace. Great theories spun by dreamers to remedy the pressing human ills have come to the front of men's minds. Great formulas came into life that promised to dissolve all trouble. Great masses of people have flocked to their banners in hopes born of misery and suffering. Nor has this great social ferment been confined to those nations that have burned with revolutions.

Now, as the storm of war, of revolution and of emotion subsides there is left even with us of the United States much unrest, much discontent with the surer forces of human advancement. To all of us, out of this crucible of actual, poignant, individual experience has come a deal of new understanding, and it is for all of us to ponder these new currents if we are to shape our future with intelligence.

Even those parts of the world that suffered less from the war have been partly infected by these ideas. Beyond this, however, many have had high hopes of civilization suddenly purified and ennobled by the sacrifices and services of the war; they had thought the fine unity of purpose gained in war would be carried into great unity of action in remedy of the faults of civilization in peace. But from concentration of every spiritual and material energy upon the single purpose of war the scene changed to the immense complexity and the many purposes of peace.

Thus there loom up certain definite underlying forces in our national life that need to be stripped of the imaginary—the transitory—and a definition should be given to the actual permanent and persistent motivation of our civilization. In contemplation of these questions we must go far deeper that the superficials of our political and economic structure, for these are but the products of our social philosophy—the machinery of our social system.

Nor is it ever amiss to review the political, economic, and spiritual principles through which our country has steadily grown in usefulness and greatness, not only to preserve them from being fouled by false notions, but more importantly that we may guide ourselves in the road to progress.

Five or six great social philosophies are at struggle in the world for ascendency. There is the Individualism of America. There is the Individualism of the more democratic states of Europe with its careful reservations of castes and classes. There are Communism, Socialism, Syndicalism, Capitalism, and finally there is Autocracy—whether by birth, by possessions, militarism, or divine right of kings. Even the Divine Right still lingers on although our lifetime has seen fully two-thirds of the earth's population, including Germany, Austria, Russia, and China, arrive at a state of angry disgust with this type of social motive power and throw it on the scrap heap.

All these thoughts are in ferment today in every country of the world. They fluctuate in ascendency with times and places. They compromise with each other in daily reaction on governments and peoples. Some of these ideas are perhaps more adapted to one race than another. Some are false, some are true. What we are interested in is their challenge to the physical and spiritual forces of America.

The partisans of some of these other brands of social schemes challenge us to comparison; and some of their partisans even among our own people are increasing in their agitation that we adopt one or another or parts of their devices in place of our tried individualism. They insist that our social foundations are exhausted, that like feudalism and autocracy, America's plan has served its purpose—that it must be abandoned.

There are those who have been left in sober doubt of our institutions or are confounded by bewildering catchwords of vivid phrases. For in this welter of discussions there is much attempt to glorify or defame social and economic forces with phrased. Nor indeed should we disregard the potency of some of these phrases in their stir to action.—"The dictatorship of the Proletariat," "Capitalistic nations," "Germany over all," and a score of others. We need only to review those that have jumped to horseback during the last ten years in order that we may be properly awed by the great social and political havoc that can be worked where the bestial instincts of hate, murder, and destruction are clothed by the demagogue in the fine terms of political idealism.

For myself, let me say at the very outset that my faith in the essential truth, strength, and vitality of the developing creed by which we have hitherto lived in this country of ours has been confirmed and deepened by the searching experiences of seven years of service in the backwash and miseries of war. Seven years of contending with economic degeneration, with social disintegration, with incessant political dislocation, with all of its seething and ferment of individual and class conflict, could but impress me with the primary motivation of social forces, and the necessity for broader thought upon their great issue to humanity. And from it all I emerge a great individualist—an unashamed individualist. But let me say also that I am an American individualist. For America has been steadily developing the ideals that constitute progressive individualism.

No doubt, individualism run riot, with no tempering principle, would provide a long category of inequalities, of tyrannies, dominations, and injustices. America, however, has tempered the whole conception of individualism by the injection of a definite principle, and from this principle it follows that attempts at domination, whether in government or in the processes of industry and commerce, are under an insistent curb. If we would have the values of individualism, their stimulation to initiative, to the development of hand and intellect, to the high development of thought and spirituality, they must be tempered with that firm and fixed ideal of American individualism—*an equality of opportunity.* If we would have these values we must soften its hardness and stimulate progress through that sense of service that lies in our people.

Therefore, it is not the individualism of other countries for which I would speak, but the individualism of America. Our individualism differs from all other because it embraces these great ideals: *that while we build our society upon the attainment of the individual, we shall safeguard to every individual an equality of opportunity to take that position in the community to which his intelligence, character, ability, and ambition entitle him; that we keep the social solution free from frozen strata of classes; that we shall stimulate efforts of*

*each individual to achievement; that through an enlarging
sense of responsibility and understanding we shall assist him
to this attainment; while he in turn must stand up to the emery
wheel of competition.*

Individualism cannot be maintained as the foundation of a
society if it looks to only legalistic justice based upon
contracts, property, and political equality. Such legalistic
safeguards are themselves not enough. In our individualism
we have long since abandoned the *laissez faire* of the 18th
Century—the notion that it is "every man for himself and the
devil take the hindmost." We abandoned that when we
adopted the ideal of equality of opportunity—the fair chance
of Abraham Lincoln. We have confirmed its abandonment in
terms of legislation, of social and economic justice,—in part
because we have learned that the foremost are not always the
best nor the hindmost the worst—and in part because we
have learned that social injustice is the destruction of justice
itself. We have learned that the impulse to production can
only be maintained at high pitch if there is a fair division of
the product. We have also learned that fair division can only
be obtained by certain restrictions on the strong and the
dominant. We have indeed gone even further in the 20th
Century with the embracement of the necessity of a greater
and broader sense of service and responsibility to others as a
part of individualism.

Whatever may be the cause with regard to Old World
individualism (and we have given more back to Europe than
we received from her) the truth that is important for us to
grasp today is that there is a world of difference between the
principles and spirit of Old World individualism and that
which we have developed in our own country.

We have, in fact, a special social system of our own. We have made it ourselves from materials brought in revolt from conditions in Europe. We have lived it; we constantly improve it; we have seldom tried to define it. It abhors autocracy and does not argue with it, but fights it. It is not capitalism, or socialism, or syndicalism, nor a cross breed of them. Like most Americans, I refuse to be damned by anybody's word-classification of it, such as "capitalism," "plutocracy," "proletariat" or "middle class," or any other, or to any kind of compartment that is based on the assumption of some group dominating somebody else.

The social Force in which I am interested is far higher and far more precious a thing than all these. It springs from something infinitely more enduring; it springs from the one source of human progress—that each individual shall be given the chance and stimulation for development of the best with which he has been endowed in heart and mind; it is the sole source of progress; it is American individualism.

The rightfulness of our individualism can rest either on philosophic, political, economic, or spiritual grounds. It can rest on the ground of being the only safe avenue to further human progress.

PHILOSOPHIC GROUNDS

On the philosophic side we can agree at once that intelligence, character, courage, and the divine spark of the human soul are alone the property of individuals. These do not lie in agreements in organizations, in institutions, in masses, or in groups. They abide alone in the individual mind and heart.

Production both of mind and hand rests upon impulses in each individual. These impulses are made of the varied forces of original instincts, motives, and acquired desires. Many of these are destructive and must be restrained through moral leadership and authority of the law and be eliminated finally by education. All are modified by a vast fund of experience and a vast plant and equipment of civilization which we pass on with increments to each succeeding generation.

The inherited instincts of self-preservation, acquisitiveness, fear, kindness, hate, curiosity, desire for self-expression, for power, for adulation, that we carry over from a thousand of generations must, for good or evil, be comprehended in a workable system embracing our accumulation of experiences and equipment. They may modify themselves with time—but in terms of generations. They differ in their urge upon different individuals. The dominant ones are selfish. But no civilization could be built or can endure solely upon the groundwork of unrestrained and unintelligent self-interest. The problem of the world is to restrain the destructive instincts while strengthening and enlarging those of altruistic character and constructive impulse—for thus we build for the future.

From the instincts of kindness, pity, fealty to family and race; the love of liberty; the mystical yearnings for spiritual things; the desire for fuller expression of the creative faculties; the impulses of service to community and nation, are moulded the ideals of our people. And the most potent force in society is its ideals. If one were to attempt to delimit the potency of instinct and ideals, it would be found that while instinct dominates in our preservation yet the great propelling force of progress is right ideals. It is true that we do not idealize the ideal; not even a single person personifies that realization. It is therefore not surprising that society, a collection of persons, a necessary maze of compromises, cannot realize it. But that it has ideals, that they revolve in a system that makes for steady advance of them is the first thing. Yet true as it is, the day has not arrived when any economic or social system will function and last if founded upon altruism alone.

With the growth of ideals through education, with the higher realization of freedom, of justice, of humanity, of service, the selfish impulses become less and less dominant, and if we ever reach the millennium, they will disappear in the aspirations and satisfactions of pure altruism. But for the next several generations we dare not abandon self-interest as a motive force to leadership and to production, lest we die.

The will-o'-the-wisp of all breeds of socialism is that they contemplate a motivation of human animals by altruism alone. It necessitates a bureaucracy of the entire population, in which having obliterated the economic stimulation of each member, the fine gradations of character and ability are to be arranged in relative authority by ballot or more likely by a Tammany Hall or a Bolshevist party, or some other form of tyranny. The proof of the futility of these ideas as a stimulation to the development and activity of the individual does not lie alone in the ghastly failure of Russia, but also lies in our own failure in attempts at nationalized industry.

Likewise the basic foundations of autocracy, whether it be class government or capitalism in the sense that a few men through unrestrained control of property determine the welfare of great numbers, is as far apart from the rightful expression of American individualism as the two poles. The will-o'-the-wisp of autocracy in any form is that it supposes that the good Lord endowed a special few with all of the divine attributes. It contemplates one human animal dealing to the other human animals his just share of the earth, of glory, and of immortality. The proof of the futility of these ideas in the development of the world does not lie alone in the grim failure of Germany, but it lies in the damage to our moral and social fabric from those who have sought economic domination in America, whether employer or employee.

We in America have had too much experience of life to fool ourselves into pretending that all men are equal in ability, in character, in intelligence, in ambition. That was part of the claptrap of the French Revolution. We have grown to understand that all we can hope to assure to the individual through government is liberty, justice, intellectual welfare, equality of opportunity, and stimulation to service.

It is in the maintenance of a society fluid to these human qualities that our individualism departs from the individualism of Europe. There can be no rise for the individual through the frozen strata of classes, or of castes, and no stratification can take place in a mass livened by the free stir of its particles. This guarding of our individualism against stratification insists not only in preserving in the social solution an equal opportunity for the able and ambitious to rise from the bottom; it also insists that the sons of the successful shall not by any mere right of birth or favor continue to occupy their father's places of power against the rise of a new generation in process of coming up from the bottom. The pioneers of our American individualism had the good sense not to reward Washington and Jefferson and Hamilton with hereditary dukedoms and fixtures in landed estates, as Great Britain rewarded Marlborough and Nelson. Otherwise, our American fields of opportunity would have been clogged with long generations inheriting their fathers' privileges without their fathers' capacity for service.

That our system had avoided the establishment and domination of class has a significant proof in the present Administration in Washington. Of the twelve men comprising the President, Vice-President, and Cabinet, nine have earned their own way in life without economic inheritance, and eight of them started with manual labor.

If we examine the impulses that carry us forward, none is so potent for progress as the yearning for individual self-expression, the desire for creation of something. Perhaps the greatest human happiness flows from personal achievement. Here lies the great urge of the constructive instinct of mankind. But it can only thrive in a society where the individual has liberty and stimulation to achievement. Nor does the community progress except through its participation in these multitudes of achievements.

Furthermore, the maintenance of productivity and the advancement of the things of the spirit depend upon the ever-renewed supply from the mass of those who can rise to leadership. Our social, economic, and intellectual progress is almost solely dependant upon the creative minds of those individuals with imaginative and administrative intelligence who create or who carry discoveries to widespread application. No race possesses more than a small percentage of these minds in a single generation. But little thought has ever been given to our racial dependency upon them. Nor that our progress is in so large a measure due to the fact that with our increased means of communication these rare individuals are today able to spread their influence over so enlarged a number of lesser capable minds as to have increased their potency a million-fold. In truth, the vastly greater productivity of the world with actually less physical labor is due to the wider spread of their influence through the discovery of these facilities. And they can arise solely through the selection that comes from the free-running mills of competition. They must be free to rise from the mass; they must be given the attraction of premiums to effort.

Leadership is a quality of the individual. It is the individual alone who can function in the world of intellect and in the field of leadership. If democracy is to secure its authorities in morals, religion, and statesmanship, it must stimulate leadership from its own mass. Human leadership cannot be replenished by selection like queen bees, by divine right or bureaucracies, but by the free rise of ability, character, and intelligence.

Even so, leadership cannot, no matter how brilliant, carry progress far ahead of the average of the mass of individual units. Progress of the nation is the sum of progress in its individuals. Acts and ideas that lead to progress are born out of the womb of the individual mind, not out of the mind of the crowd. The crowd only feels: it has no mind of its own which can plan. The crowd is credulous, it destroys, it consumes, it hates, and it dreams—but it never builds. It is one of the most profound and important of exact psychological truths that man in the mass does not think but only feels. The mob functions only in a world of emotion. The demagogue feeds on mob emotions and his leadership is the leadership of emotion, not the leadership of intellect and progress. Popular desires are no criteria to the real need; they can be determined only by deliberative consideration, by education, by conservative leadership.

SPIRITUAL PHASES

Our social and economic system cannot march toward better days unless it is inspired by things of the spirit. It is here that the higher purposes of individualism must find their sustenance. Men do not live by bread alone. Nor is individualism merely a stimulus to production and the road to liberty; it alone admits the universal divine inspiration of every human soul. I may repeat that the divine spark does not lie in agreements, in organizations, in institutions, in masses or in groups. Spirituality with its faith, its hope, its charity, can be increased by each individual's own effort. And in proportion as each individual increases his own store of spirituality, in that proportion increases the idealism of democracy.

For centuries, the human race believed that divine inspiration rested in a few. The result was blind faith in religious hierarchies, the Divine Right of Kings. The world has been disillusioned of this belief that divinity rests in any special group or class whether it be through a creed, a tyranny of kinds or of proletariat. Our individualism insists upon the divine in each human being. It rest upon the firm faith that the divine spark can be awakened in every heart. It was the refusal to compromise these things that led to the migration of those religious groups who so largely composed our forefathers. Our diversified religious faiths are the apotheosis of spiritual individualism.

The vast multiplication of voluntary organizations for altruistic purposes are themselves proud of the ferment of spirituality, service, and mutual responsibility. These associations for the advancement of public welfare, improvement, morals, charity, public opinion, health, the clubs and societies for recreation and intellectual advancement, represent something moving at a far greater depth than "joining." They represent the widespread aspiration for mutual advancement, self-expression, and neighborly helpfulness. Moreover, today when we rehearse our own individual memories of success, we find that none gives us such comfort as memory of service given. Do we not refer to our veterans as service men? Do not our merchants and business men pride themselves in something of service given beyond the price of their goods? When we traverse the glorious deeds of our fathers, we today never enumerate those acts that were not rooted in the soil of service. Those whom we revere are those who triumphed in service, for from them comes the uplift of the human heart and the uplift of the human mind.

While there are forces in the growth of our individualism which must be curbed with vigilance, yet there are no less glorious spiritual forces growing within that promise for the future. There is developing in our people a new valuation of individuals and of groups and of nations. It is a rising vision of service. Indeed if I were to select the social force that above all others has advanced sharply during these past years of suffering, it is that of service—service to those with whom we come in contact, service to the nation, and service to the world itself. If we examine the great mystical forces of the past seven years we find this great spiritual force poured out by our people as never before in the history of the world—the ideal of service.

Just now we are weakened by the feeling of failure of immediate realization of the great ideas and hopes that arose through the exaltation of war. War by its very nature sets loose chaotic forces of which the results cannot be foretold or anticipated. The insensitiveness to the brutalities of physical violence, and all the spiritual dislocations of war, have left us, at the moment, poorer. The amount of serenity and content in the world is smaller.

The spiritual reaction after the war has been in part the fruit of some illusions during those five years. In the presence of unity of purpose and the mystic emotions of war, many men came to believe that salvation lay in mass and group action. They have seen the spiritual and material mobilization of nations, of classes, and groups, for sacrifice and service; they have conceived that real human progress can be achieved by working on "the psychology of the people"— by the "mass mind;" they yielded to leadership without reservation; they conceived that this leadership could continue without tyranny; they have forgotten that permanent spiritual progress lies with the individual.

ECONOMIC PHASES

That high and increasing standard of living and comfort should be first of considerations in public mind and in government needs no apology. We have long since realized that the basis of an advancing civilization must be a high and growing standard of living for all of the people, not for a single class; that education, food, clothing, housing, and the spreading use of what we so often term nonessentials, are the real fertilizers of the soil from which spring the finer flowers of life. The economic development of the past fifty years has lifted the general standard of comfort far beyond the dreams of our forefathers. The only road to further advance in the standard of living is by greater invention, greater elimination of waste, greater production and better distribution of commodities and services, for by increasing their ratio to our numbers and dividing them justly we each will have more of them.

The superlative value of individualism through its impulse to production, its stimulation to invention, has, so far as I know, never been denied. Criticism of it has lain in its wastes but more importantly in its failures of equitable sharing of the product. In our country these contentions are mainly over the division to each of his share of the comforts and luxuries, for none of us is either hungry or cold or without a place to lay his head—and we have much besides. In less than four decades we have added electric lights, plumbing, telephones, gramophones, automobiles, and what not in wide diffusion to our standards of living. Each in turn began as a luxury, each in turn has become so commonplace that seventy or eighty per cent of our people participate in them.

To all practical souls there is little use in quarreling over the share of each of us until we have something to divide. So long as we maintain our individualism we will have increasing quantities to share and we shall have time and leisure and taxes with which to fight our proper sharing of the "surplus." The income tax returns show that this surplus is a minor part of our total production after taxes are paid. Some of this "surplus" must be set aside for rewards to saving for stimulation of proper effort to skill, to leadership and invention—therefore the dispute is in reality over much less than the total of such "surplus." While there should be no minimizing of a certain fringe of injustices in sharing the results of production or in the wasteful use made by some in their share, yet there is vastly wider field for gains to all of us through cheapening the costs of production and distribution through the eliminating of their wastes, from increasing the volume of product by each and every one doing his utmost, than will ever come to us even if we can think out a method of abstract justice in sharing which did not stifle production of the total product.

It is a certainty we are confronted with a population in such numbers as can only exist by production attuned to a pitch in which the slightest reduction of the impulse to produce will at once create misery and want. If we throttle the fundamental impulses of man our production will decay. The world in this hour is witnessing the most overshadowing tragedy of ten centuries in the heart-breaking life-and-death struggle with starvation by a nation with a hundred and fifty millions of people. In Russia under the new tyranny a group, in pursuit of social theories, have destroyed the primary self-interest impulse of the individual to production.

Although socialism in a nation-wide application has now proved itself with rivers of blood and inconceivable misery to be an economic and spiritual fallacy and has wrecked itself finally upon the rocks of destroyed production and moral degeneracy, I believe it to have been necessary for the world to have had this demonstration. Great theoretic and emotional ideas have arisen before in the world's history and have in more than mere material bankruptcy deluged the world with fearful losses of life. A purely philosophical view might be that in the long run humanity has to try every way, even precipices, in finding the road to betterment.

But those are utterly wrong who say that individualism has as its only end the acquisition and preservation of private property—the selfish snatching and hoarding of the common product. Our American individualism, indeed, is only in part an economic creed. It aims to provide opportunity for self-expression, not merely economically, but spiritually as well.

Private property is not a fetich in America. The crushing of the liquor trade without a cent of compensation, with scarcely even a discussion of it, does not bear out the notion that we gave property rights any headway over human rights. Our development of individualism shows an increasing tendency to regard right of property not as an object in itself, but in the light of a useful and necessary instrument in stimulation of initiative to the individual; not only stimulation to him that he may gain personal comfort, security in life, protection to his family, but also because individual accumulation and ownership is a basis of selection to leadership in administration of the tools of industry and commerce. It is where dominant private property is assembled in the hands of the groups who control the state that the individual begins to feel capital as an oppressor. Our American demand for equality of opportunity is a constant militant check upon capital becoming a thing to be feared. Out of fear we sometimes even go too far and stifle the reproductive use of capital by crushing the initiative that makes for its creation.

Some discussion of the legal limitations we have placed upon economic domination is given later on, but it is desirable to mention here certain potent forces in our economic life that are themselves providing their own correction to domination.

The domination by arbitrary individual ownership is disappearing because the works of today are steadily growing more and more beyond the resources of any one individual, and steadily taxation will reduce relatively excessive individual accumulations. The number of persons in partnership through division of ownership among many stockholders is steadily increasing—thus 100,000 to 200,000 partners in a single concern are not uncommon. The overwhelmingly largest portion of our mobile capital is that of our banks, insurance companies, building and loan associations, and the vast majority of all this is the aggregated small savings of our people, Thus large capital is steadily becoming more and more a mobilization of the savings of the small holder—the actual people themselves—and its administration becomes at once more sensitive to the moral opinions of the people in order to attract their support. The directors and managers of large concerns, themselves employees of these great groups of individual stockholders, or policy holders, reflect a spirit of community responsibility.

Large masses of capital can only find their market for service or production to great numbers of the same kind of people that they employ and they must therefore maintain confidence in their public responsibilities in order to retain their customers. In times when the products of manufacture were mostly luxuries to the average of the people, the condition of their employees was of no such interest to their customers as when they cater to employees in general. Of this latter, no greater proofs need exist that the efforts of many large concerns directly dependent upon public good will to restrain prices in scarcity—and the very general desire to yield a measure of service with the goods sold. Another phase of this same development in administration of capital is the growth of a sort of institutional sense in many large business enterprises. The encouragement of solidarity in all grades of their employees in the common service and common success, the sense of mutuality with the prosperity of the community are both vital developments in individualism.

There has been in the last thirty years an extraordinary growth of organizations for advancement of ideas in the community for mutual cooperation and economic objectives—the chambers of commerce, trade associations, labor unions, and what not. There are indeed variable mixtures of altruism and self-interest. Nevertheless, in these groups the individual finds an opportunity for self-expression and participation in the moulding of ideas, a field for training and the stepping stones for leadership.

The number of leaders in local and national life whose opportunity to service came through these associations has become now of more importance than those through the direct lines of political and religious organization.

At times these groups come into sharp conflict and often enough charge each other with crimes against public interest. They do contain faults; if they develop into warring interests, if they dominate legislators and intimidate public officials, if they are to be a new setting of tyranny, then they will destroy the foundation of individualism. Our Government will then drift into the hands of timorous mediocrities dominated by groups until we shall become a syndicalist nation on a gigantic scale. On the other hand, each group is a realization of greater mutuality of interest, each contains some element of public service and each in a school of public responsibility. In the main, the same forces that permeate the nation at large eventually permeate these groups. The sense of service, a growing sense of responsibility, and the sense of constructive opposition to domination, constantly recall them in their responsibilities as well as their privileges. In the end, no group can dominate the nation and few successes in imposing the will of any group is its sure death warrant.

Today business organization is moving strongly toward cooperation. There are in the cooperative great hopes that we can even gain in individuality, equality of opportunity, and an enlarged field for initiative, and at the same time reduce many of the great wastes of overreckless competition in production and distribution. Those who either congratulate themselves or those who fear that cooperation is an advance toward socialism need neither rejoice or worry. Cooperation in its current economic sense represents the initiative of self-interest blended with a sense of service, for nobody belongs to a cooperative who is not striving to sell his products or services for more or striving to buy from others for less or striving to make his income more secure. Their members are furnishing the capital for extension of their activities just as effectively as if they did it in corporate form and they are simply transferring the profit principle from joint return to individual return. Their only success lies where they eliminate waste either in production or distribution—and they can do neither if they destroy individual initiative. Indeed, this phase of development of our individualism promises to become the dominant note of its 20th Century expansion. But it will thrive only in so far as it can construct leadership and a sense of service, and so long as it preserves the initiative and safeguards the individuality of its members.

The economic system which is the result of our individualism is not a frozen organism. It moves rapidly in its form of organization under the impulse of initiative of our citizens, of growing science, or larger production and of constantly cheapening distribution.

A great test of the soundness of a social system must be its ability to evolve within itself those orderly shifts in its administration that enable it to apply the new tools of social, economic, and intellectual progress, and to eliminate the malign forces that may grow in the application of these tools. When we were almost wholly an agricultural people our form of organization and administration, both in the governmental and economic fields, could be simple. With the enormous shift in growth to industry and commerce we have erected organisms that each generation had denounced as Frankensteins, yet the succeeding generation proves them to be controllable and useful. The growth of corporate organizations, of our banking systems, or our railways, or our electrical power, of our farm cooperatives, of our trade unions, of our trade associations, and of a hundred other indeed develops both beneficent and malign forces. The timid become frightened. But our basic social ideas march through the new things in the end. Our demagogues, of both radical and standpat breed, thrive on demands for the destruction of one or another of these organizations as the only solution for their defects, yet progress requires only a guardianship of the vital principles of our individualism with its safeguard of true equality of opportunity in them.

POLITICAL PHASES

It is not the primary purpose of this essay to discuss our political organization. Democracy is merely the mechanism which individualism invented as a device that would carry on the necessary political work of its social organization. Democracy arises out of individualism and prospers through it alone.

Without question, there exists, almost all over the world, unprecedented disquietude at the functioning of government itself. It is in part the dreamy social ferment of war emotion. It is in part the aftermath of a period when the Government was everything and the individual nothing, from which there is much stimulation to two schools of thought: one that all human ills can be cured by governmental regulation, and the other that all regulation is a sin.

During the war, the mobilization of every effort, the destruction of the normal demand and the normal avenues of distribution, required a vast excursion over the deadline of individualism in order that we might secure immediate results. Its continuation would have destroyed the initiative of our people and undermined all real progress. We are slowly getting back, but many still aspire to these supposed short cuts to the millennium.

Much of our discontent takes the form of resentment against the inequalities in the distribution of the sacrifices of war. Both silently and vocally there is complaint that while some died, others ran no risk, and yet others profited. For these complaints there is adequate justification. The facts are patent. However, no conceivable human intelligence would be able to manage the conduct of war so as to see that all sacrifices and burdens should be distributed equitably. War is destruction and we should blame war for its injustices, not a social system whose object is construction. The submergence of the individual, however, in the struggle of the race could be but temporary—its continuance through the crushing of individual action and its inequities would, if for no other reason, destroy the foundations of our civilization.

Looked at as the umpire in our social system, our Government has maintained an equality before the law and a development of legal justice and an authority in restraint of evil instincts that support this social system and its ideals so far as the imperfections of developing human institutions permit. It has gone the greatest distance of any government toward maintaining an equality of franchise; an equality of entrance to public office, and government by the majority. It has succeeded far beyond all other in those safeguards of equality of opportunity through education, public information, and the open channels of free speech and free press. It is, however, to chart the course of government in dealing with the abstract problems of order, political liberty, and stimulation to intellectual and moral advancement than it is to chart its relations to the economic seas. These seas are new and only partly discovered or explored.

Our Government's greatest troubles and failures are in the economic field. Forty years ago the contact of the individual with the Government had its largest expression in the sheriff or policeman, and in debates over political equality. In those happy days the Government offered but small interference with the economic life of the citizen. But with the vast development of industry and the train of regulating functions of the national and municipal government that followed from it; with the recent vast increase in taxation due to the war;— the Government has become through its relations to economic life the most potent force for maintenance or destruction of our American individualism.

The entrance of the Government began strongly three decades ago, when our industrial organization began to move powerfully in the direction of consolidation of enterprise. We found in the course of this development that equality of opportunity and its corollary, individual initiative, was being throttled by the concentration of control of industry and service, and thus the economic domination of groups bullied over the nation. At this time, particularly, we were threatened with a form of autocracy of economic power. Our mass of regulation of public utilities and our legislation against restraint of trade is the monument to our intent to preserve an equality of opportunity. This regulation is itself proof that we have gone a long way toward the abandonment of the "capitalism" of Adam Smith.

Day by day we learn more as to the practical application of restrictions against economic and political domination. We sometimes lag behind in the correction of those forces that would override liberty, justice, and equality of opportunity, but the principle is so strong within us that domination of the few will not be tolerated. These restraints must keep pace with the growing complexity of our economic organization, but they need tuning to our social system if they would not take us into great dangers. As we build up our powers of production through the advancing application of science we create new forces with which men may dominate—railway, power, oil, and what not. They may produce temporary blockades upon equality of opportunity.

To curb the forces in business which would destroy equality of opportunity and yet maintain the initiative and creative faculties of our people are the twin objects we must attain. To preserve the former we must regulate that type of activity that would dominate. To preserve the latter, the Government must keep out of production and distribution of commodities and services. This is the deadline between our system and socialism. Regulation to prevent domination and unfair practices, yet preserving rightful initiative, are in keeping with our social foundations. Nationalization of industry or business is their negation.

When we come to the practical problems of government in relation to these economic questions the test lies in two directions: Does this act safeguard an equality of opportunity? Does it maintain the initiative of the people? For in the first must lie the deadline against domination, and in the second the deadline in preservation of individualism against socialism. Excluding the temporary measures of the war, the period of regulation has now been long enough with us to begin to take stock of its effect on our social system. It has been highly beneficial, but it has also developed weaknesses in the throttling of proper initiative that require some revision. We have already granted relief to labor organizations and to agriculture from some forms of regulation. There is, however, a large field of cooperative possibilities far outside agriculture that are needlessly hampered.

The most important of considerations in any attempt to pass judgement upon social systems is whether we maintain within them permanent and continuous motivation toward progress. These forces must be of two orders, one spiritual and the other economic.

We may discover the situation in our own social system either by an analysis of the forces that are today in motion or by noting the strides of progress over the century or over the last ten years. By a consideration of the forces that move us we can see whether its virility is maintained; and by the touchstone of time we can find out whether these forces have been powerful enough to overcome the malign influences that would lessen the well-being of our system.

If we should survey the fundamentals of our civilization from the point of view of its progress by the test of time, we can find much for satisfaction and assurance. It is unnecessary to recount the values of economic individualism in simulation to invention; large constructive vision; intensity in production with decreased physical effort; our increased standards of living and comfort. It is of course easy to enumerate our great economic progress, but the progress of the social forces that will sustain economic progress in infinitely more important—for upon them depends the real future of our people. Education in its many phases has made much advance. The actual equipment, the character of instruction, the numbers reached, period of instruction—show improvement with every decade. Public opinion has become of steadily increasing potency and reliability in its reaction. The great strides in development of processes and equipment for production and distribution are being followed by increasing devotion to human factors in their execution. Moral standards of business and commerce are improving; vicious city governments are less in number; invisible government has greatly diminished; public conscience is penetrating deeper and deeper; the rooting up of wrong grows more vigorous; the agencies for their exposure and remedy grow more numerous, and above all is the growing sense of service. Many people confuse the exposure of wrongs which were below the surface with degeneration; their very exposure is progress. Some accredit the exposures of failure in our government and business as evidence of standards of a lower order than in some other nations. A considerable experience leads me to the conviction that while we do wash our dirty linen in public most others never wash it.

It is easy to arraign any existing institution. Men can rightly be critical because things have happened that never ought to happen. That our social system contains faults no one disputes. One can recite the faulty results of our system at great length; the spirit of lawlessness; the uncertainty of unemployment in some callings; the deadening effect of certain repetitive processes of manufacture; the 12-hour day in a few industries; unequal voice in bargaining for wage in some employment; arrogant domination by some employers and some labor leaders; child labor in some states; inadequate instruction in some areas; unfair competition in some industries; some fortunes excessive far beyond the needs of stimulation to initiative; survivals of religious intolerance; political debauchery of some cities; weakness in our government structure. Most of these occur locally in certain regions and certain industries and must cause every thinking person to regret and to endeavor. But they are becoming steadily more local. That they are recognized and condemned is a long way on the road to progress.

One of the difficulties in social thought is to find the balance of perspective. A single crime does not mean a criminal community. It is easy to point out undernourished, overworked, uneducated children, children barred from the equality of opportunity that our ideals stand for. It is easy to point out the luxurious petted and spoiled children with favored opportunity in every community. But if we take the whole thirty-five millions of children of the United States, it would be a gross exaggeration to say that a million of them suffer from any of these injustices. This is indeed a million too many, but it is the thirty-four million that tests the system with the additional touchstone of whether there are forces in motivation which are insistently and carefully working for the amelioration of the one million. Its by-products of endowed loafers, or hoodlums, at respective ends of the economic scale, are indeed spectacular faults. Yet any analysis of the 105,000,000 of us would show that we harbor less than a million of either rich or impecunious loafers. If we measure our people by scales of other civilized peoples, we also find consolation. We have a distaste for the very expression of "class," but if we would use European scales of "classes" we would find that above their scale of "lower classes" we have in equivalent comfort, morality, understanding, and intelligence fully eighty per cent of our native-born whites. No European state will lay claim to thirty per cent of this order. Does this not mean that we have been gaining something?

I do not conceive that any man, or body of men, could ever be capable of drafting a plan that would solve these multiple difficulties in advance. Moreover, if we continue to advance we will find new difficulties and weaknesses as the by-product of progress—but to be overcome.

THE FUTURE

Individualism has been the primary force of American civilization for three centuries. It is our sort of individualism that has supplied the motivation of America's political, economic, and spiritual institutions in all these years. It has proved its ability to develop its institutions with the changing scene. Our very form of government is the product of the individualism of our people, the demand for an equal opportunity, for a fair chance.

The American pioneer is the epic expression of that individualism, and the pioneer spirit is the response to the challenge of opportunity, to the challenge of nature, to the challenge of life, to the call of the frontier. That spirit need never die for lack of something for it to achieve. There will always be a frontier to conquer or to hold as long as men think, plan, and dare. Our American individualism has received much of its character from our contacts with the forces of nature on a new continent. It evolved government without official emissaries to show the way; it plowed and sowed two score of great states; it built roads, bridges, railways, cities; it carried forward every attribute of high civilization over a continent. The days of the pioneer are not over. There are continents of human welfare for which we have penetrated only the coastal plain. The great continent of science is as yet explored only on its borders, and it is only the pioneer who will penetrate the frontier in the quest for new worlds to conquer. The very genius of our institutions has been given to them by a pioneer spirit. Our individualism is rooted in our very nature. It is based on conviction born of experience. Equal opportunity, the demand for a fair chance, became the formula of American individualism because it is the method of American achievement.

After the absorption of the great plains of the West came the era of industrial development with the new complex for forces that it has brought us. Now haltingly, but with more surety and precision than ever before and with a more conscious understanding of our mission, we are finding solution of these problems arising from new conditions, for the forces of our social system can compass and comprise these.

Our individualism in no middle ground between autocracy—whether of birth, economic or class origin—and socialism. Socialism of different varieties may have something to recommend it as an intellectual stop-look-and-listen sign, more especially for Old World societies. But it contains only destruction to the forces that make progress in our social system. Nor does salvation come by any device for concentration of power, whether political or economic, for both are equally reversions to Old World autocracy in new garments.

Salvation will not come to us out of the wreckage of individualism. What we need today is steady devotion to a better, brighter, broader individualism—an individualism that carries increasing responsibility and service to our fellows.

Our need is not for a way out but for a way forward. We found our way out three centuries ago when our forefathers left Europe for these shores, to set up here a commonwealth conceived in liberty and dedicated to the development of individuality.

There are malign social forces other than our failures that would destroy our progress. There are the equal dangers both of reaction and radicalism. The perpetual howl of radicalism is that it is the sole voice of liberalism—that devotion to social progress is its field alone. These men would assume that all reform and human advance must come through government. They have forgotten that progress must come from the steady lift of the individual and that the measure of national idealism and progress is the quality of idealism in the individual. The most trying support of radicalism comes from the timid or dishonest minds that shrink from facing the result of radicalism itself but are devoted to defense of radicalism as proof of a liberal mind. Most theorists who denounce our individualism as a social basis seem to have a passion for ignorance of its constructive ideals.

An even greater danger is the destructive criticism of minds too weak or too partisan to harbor constructive ideas. For such, criticism is based upon the distortion of perspective or cunning misrepresentation. There is never danger from the radical himself until the structure and confidence of society has been undermined by the enthronement of destructive criticism. Destructive criticism can certainly lead to revolution unless there are those willing to withstand the malice that flows in return from refutation. If has been well said that revolution is no summer thunderstorm clearing the atmosphere. In modern society it is a tornado leaving in its path the destroyed homes of million with their dead women and children.

There are also those who insist that the future must be a repetition of the past; that ideas are dangerous, that ideals are freaks.

To find that fine balance which links the future with the past, whose vision is of men and not of tools that possesses the courage to construct rather than to criticize—this is our need. There is no oratory so easy, no writing so trenchant and vivid as the phrase-making of criticism and malice—there is none so difficult as inspiration to construction.

We cannot ever afford to rest at ease in the comfortable assumption that right ideas always prevail by some virtue of their own. In the long run they do. But there can be and there have been periods of centuries when the world slumped back toward darkness merely because great masses of men became impregnated with wrong ideas and wrong social philosophies. The declines of civilization have been born of wrong ideas. Most of the wars of the world, including the recent one, have been fought by the advocates of contrasting ideas of social philosophy.

The primary safeguard of American individualism is an understanding of it; of faith that it is the most precious possession of American civilization, and a willingness courageously to test every process of national life upon the touchstone of this basic social premise. Development of the human institutions and of science and of industry have been long chains of trial and error. Our public relations to them and to other phases of our national life can be advanced in no other way than by a willingness to experiment in the remedy of our social faults. The failures and unsolved problems of economic and social life can be corrected; they can be solved within our social theme and under no other system. The solution is a matter of will to find solution; of a sense of duty as well as of a sense of right and citizenship. No one who buys "bootleg" whiskey can complain of gunmen and hoodlumism.

Humanity has a long road to perfection, but we of America can make sure progress if we will preserve our individualism, if we will preserve and stimulate the initiative of our people, if we will build up our insistence and safeguards to equality of opportunity, if we will glorify service as a part of our national character. Progress will march if we hold an abiding faith in the intelligence, the initiative, the character, the courage, and the divine touch in the individual. We can safeguard these ends if we give each individual that opportunity for which the spirit of America stands. We can make a social system as perfect as our generation merits and one that will be received in gratitude by our children.

The Challenge to Liberty

Introduction

For the first time in two generations the American people are faced with the primary issue of humanity and all government—the issue of human liberty.

THE WORLD-WIDE ATTACK UPON LIBERTY

Not only in the United States, but throughout the world, the whole philosophy of individual liberty is under attack. In haste to bring under control the sweeping social forces unleashed by the political and economic dislocations of the World War, by the tremendous advances in productive technology during the last quarter-century, by the failure to march with a growing sense of justice, peoples and governments are blindly wounding, even destroying those fundamental human liberties which have been the foundation and the inspiration of progress since the Middle Ages.

The great question before the American people is not whether these dislocations and abuses can be mastered and powerful forces organized and directed to human welfare, but whether they can be organized by free men. We have to determine now whether, under the pressures of the hour, we must cripple or abandon the heritage of liberty for some new philosophy which must mark the passing of freedom.

THE PRINCIPLES OF LIBERTY

Who may define Liberty? It is far more than Independence of a nation. It is not a catalogue of political "rights." Liberty is a thing of the spirit—to be free to worship, to think, to hold opinions, and to speak without fear—free to challenge wrong and oppression with surety of justice. Liberty conceives that the mind and spirit of men can be free only if the individual is free to choose his own calling, to develop his talents, to win and to keep a home sacred from intrusion, to rear children in ordered security. It holds he must be free to earn, to spend, to save, to accumulate property that may give protection in old age and to loved ones.

It holds both in principle and in world experience that these intellectual and spiritual freedoms cannot thrive except where there are also these economic freedoms. It insists equally upon protections to all these freedoms or there is no Liberty. It therefore holds that no man, no group, may infringe upon the liberties of others. It demands freedom from frozen barriers of class, and equal opportunity for every boy and girl to win that place in the community to which their abilities and character entitle them. It holds that these liberties and securities to constructive initiative and enterprise alone assure the immense need of material, moral, and spiritual achievements of men.

There are stern obligations upon those who would hold these liberties—self-restraint, insistence upon truth, order, and justice, vigilance of opinion, and co-operation in the common welfare.

THE PHILOSOPHY OF LIBERALISM

In every generation men and women of many nations have died that the human spirit may be thus free. In our race, at Plymouth Rock, at Lexington, at Valley Forge, at Yorktown, at New Orleans, at every step of the Western frontier, at Gettysburg, at San Juan Hill, in the Argonne, are the graves of Americans who died for this purpose.

From these sacrifices and in the consummation of these liberties there grew a great philosophy of society—Liberalism. The high tenant of this philosophy is that Liberty is an endowment from the Creator of every individual man and woman upon which no power, whether economic or political, can encroach, and that not even government may deny. And herein it challenges all other philosophies of society and government; and all others, both before and since, insist that the individual has no such unalienable rights, that he is but the servant of the state. Liberalism holds that man is master of the state, not the servant; that the sole purpose of government is to nurture and assure these liberties. All others insist that Liberty is not a God-given right; that the state is the master of the man. Herein is the widest divergence of social and governmental concepts known to mankind. No man long holds his freedom under a government which claims men's liberties. The government cannot exist or continue unless it be of despotic powers. The whole of human experience has shown that.

And this devotion to freedom is not an abstraction, for Liberalism holds that it is solely through the release of the constructive instinct and aspirations of man that society may move forward to its primary purpose. That high purpose is human betterment. Its distinction in American life is its ideal for betterment of all the people.

THE AMERICAN SYSTEM

Out of our philosophy grew the American Constitutional system where the obligation to promote the common welfare was mandatory and could be made effective; wherein was embodied in its very framework the denial of the right of the government itself or of any group, any business, or any class to infringe upon essential liberties; wherein the majority was to rule; wherein government was to be "of laws and not of men;" whereby the individual was guaranteed the just protection of these rights by its tribunals— the structure of American Democracy.

Out of these ideals, under this philosophy, and through this structure we have developed the principles and forms of our social, economic, and governmental life—the American System.

The rise of our race under it marks the high tide of a thousand years of human struggle. Upon it our country has grown to greatness and has led the world in the emancipation of men. When these boundaries of Liberty are overstepped, America will cease to be American.

From the creativeness of mankind's liberated mind and spirit has come the host of ideas, discoveries, and inventions with their freight of comforts and opportunities. And with all of them has come a burden of difficult problems to Liberty. Today, these complexities, added to the aftermaths of war, loom large, and the voices of discouragement join with the voices of other social faiths to assert that an irreconcilable conflict has arisen in which Liberty must be sacrificed upon the alter of the Machine Age. But Liberty is a living force, expanding to every new vision of humanity, and from its very dynamic freedom of mind and thought comes the conquest of its ceaseless problems.

Our system has at all times had to contend with internal encroachments upon Liberty. Greed in economic agencies invades it from the Right, and greed for power in bureaucracy and government infringes it from the Left. Its battles against betrayal of trust, business exploitation, and all forms of economic tyranny have long demonstrated that it was no system of *laissez faire*. Its battles against the spoils system or the expansion of bureaucracy have long demonstrated its live sense of opposition to the subtle approach of political tyranny.

I should indeed be glad to find a short cut to end the immensities of human problems. I have no word of criticism but rather great sympathy with those who honestly search human experience and human thought for some easy way out, where human selfishness has no opportunities, where freedom requires no safeguards, where justice required no striving, where bread comes without contention and with little sweat. Such dreams are not without value and one could join in them with satisfaction but for the mind troubled be recollection of human frailty, the painful human advance through history, the long road, which humanity still has to travel to economic and social perfections, and but for the woeful confirmations which the world has given of the failure of idealism alone without the compass of experience.

It is now claimed by large and vocal groups, both in and out of government, that Liberty has failed; that emergency encroachments upon its principles should be made permanent. Thereby are created the most urgent issues: first, whether we must submit to some other system by which the fundamentals of Liberty are sacrificed; and second, whether, even if we make these sacrifices, we shall not defeat the hope and progress of humanity. These are not partisan issues. They are the great issues of American life.

It is my hope to show that to resume the path of Liberty is not to go backward; it is definitely to choose the sole path of progress instead of following the will-o'-the-wisps which lead either to the swamps of primitive greed or to political tyranny. The hope of America and the world is to regenerate Liberty with its responsibilities and its obligations—not to abandon it.

On other occasions I have commented upon the perversion and assumption of the term "liberalism" by theories of every ilk—whether National Regimentation, Fascism, Socialism, Communism, or what not.[1] I have pointed out that these philosophies are the very negation of American Liberalism.

---

[1] Social, political, and governmental terms are so subject to perversions from their basic concepts as to lead to confusion unless they are first defined. In this examination I shall use the term *Liberty* as defined on page 1. I shall use *Liberalism* as the philosophy of Liberty as outlined in this introduction, which is the sense in which it was born and applied in our own national life, and in which it is truly used throughout the world. It American development I shall define as *American Liberalism*. I shall define our system of social, economic, and governmental life that had developed under this philosophy as the *American System*. I shall use use synonymously the term *Liberty* with *American Liberty*. The Term *Freedom* is used in the general or in its patriotic sense. It often has less personal quality and represents less of a definite social philosophy than Liberty.

   Philosophically the Liberals are often contrasted with Conservatives and Radicals. The original "Conservatives" were those who believed that human rights sprang from the State or the Sovereign—a curious analogy to many of the modern Radicals who daily claim to be Liberals under the cloak of Socialism or under the expansion of bureaucracies which would dictate the lives of men. These have simply shifted from Divine Right of Kings to Divine Right of Bureaucracies. In this sense the Radicals of today are the Conservatives of yesterday.

Liberalism is not the possession of any political party. The belief in Liberalism, the acceptance of it as a positive philosophy, does not designate a person either as a Republican or a Democrat any more than does his belief in Christianity.

THE PURPOSE OF THIS BOOK

It is the purpose of this examination, therefore, upon behalf of human liberty, to survey briefly the movement of revolution through the world since the Great War, and the method of overthrow of Liberalism; to recall our American heritage, the growth of our Liberty, the forces in human nature and human behavior which govern economic life, the restraints and ideals of the system of ordered Liberty, the achievements of the American System; to analyze from an American point of view the alternate systems of society; to examine our own abuses of Liberty; to review the purposes of American life; to consider constructively, not a detailed program, but the method through which alone we can solve national problems.

The creed of Liberty could be shortly and simply stated, but the complexity of material life and above all the immensity of the issue today necessitate its exhaustive examination from many angles. It may be felt that there are occasional repetitions of test, but if we make a searching examination we must review many events, many problems, and many proposals with the same lamp.

With the ordinary or technical economic or governmental problems, important as they are, I shall be here concerned only incidentally as they affect Liberty. It is enough for one brief book to outline their political and social repercussions on what is above all the crucial consideration—that is Liberty itself.

Over a period of twenty years I have been honored by my country with positions where contention with the forces of social disintegration was my continued duty. I should be untrue to that service did I not raise my voice in Protest, not at reform, but at the threat of the eclipse of Liberty.

Nor is it my purpose to criticize individual men. This is solely the issue and will be met by honest men as an issue. For once again the United States of American faces the test whether "a nation so conceived and so dedicated can long endure."

Chapter 1

Revolutions from Liberty

Some twelve years ago, after seven years of intimate and poignant participation in the backwash of war and revolution, I published a small book on the development and ideals of *American Individualism.* That essay was devoted to a survey of the American System from the point of view of the individual, in contrast with the individual under other social philosophies, rather than to the broader aspect of government.

REVOLUTIONS OVER THE WORLD

At that time the scene was the post-war sweep of revolution over one-third of the world. Great theories spun by dreamers to remedy pressing human ills then had come to the front of men's minds; magic formulas had sprung to life with the promise of dissolving all troubles; great masses of people had flocked to these new banners in hopes born of misery and despair; and, as the storm of war and revolution and overwrought emotions subsided, there was left with us of the United States even then much unrest, much discontent with the sure forces of human advancement.

THEIR CAUSES

In that essay I stated that to all of us, out of this crucible of actual, poignant, individual experience, had come a depth of new understanding. It was for all of us to ponder these new currents if we were to shape our future with intelligence. After recounting the great social philosophies which then were struggling for ascendence in prostrated Europe, this essay continued:

> The partisans of some of these other brands of social schemes challenge us to comparison; and some of their partisans even among our own people are increasing in their agitation that we adopt one or another or parts of their devices in place of our tried individualism. They insist that our social foundations are exhausted, that like feudalism and autocracy, America's plan has served its purpose—that it must be abandoned.

> There are those who have been left in sober doubt of our institutions or are confounded by bewildering catchwords of vivid phrases. For in this welter of discussions there is much attempt to glorify or defame social and economic forces with phrases. Nor indeed should we disregard the potency of some of these phrases in their stir to action....

> For myself, let me say at the very outset that my faith in the essential truth, strength, and vitality of the developing creed by which we have hitherto lived in this country of ours has been confirmed and deepened by the searching experiences of seven years of service in the backwash and miseries of war.

Humanity has had another twelve years of wracking experience since that essay was written. From the furnaces of war it has been plunged into the furnaces of economic disorder. The lingering effects of the stupendous destruction of the war; the economic dislocations of the peace; the vast speculation founded on the increasing effort to avoid payment of both private and public debt through inflation and manipulation of currencies; the efforts to make some other nation pay governmental debts; the explosive fuel of nationalism; the unassimilated scientific discoveries and inventions; all these have brought the Great Depression, with its vast unemployment and untold misery.

Stupendous problems have been thrust upon us, for which our social system is blamed rather than the shocks of war and of its peace. The overcoming of these immediate emergencies has much delayed the solutions of the world's constant problems of progress.

NEW PHILOSOPHIES

Still more new social philosophies have sprung to life in these twelve years; further test of the older ones have gained in these fierce crucibles of human experience. Fascism, Naziism have come into actual being. New Utopias have been invented, new slogans and phrases have led great masses of suffering people first this way and then that. New revolutions have burned over peoples and even swept again over old burned fields.

THE PATTERN OF MODERN REVOLUTIONS

The revolutions of democracy from autocratic governments in a large part of the civilized world which were the first products of war have now been mostly reversed. In many other countries also revolutions have replaced older liberal governments by so-called "authoritarianism" governments—that is, near dictatorship or dictatorship—until far less of humanity enjoys the blessings of freedom than a score of years ago. But beyond all this Liberalism is now under beleaguered attack even in the great countries of its origins.

These modern revolutions do not necessarily imply civil war or the killing of people. They more often force back the weakened liberal institutions by clipping, bending, or atrophying of the old frameworks into new forms and purposes.

Revolution in government is a hard term to define. Too often we use it colloquially for normal change. Any definition of revolution in democracies implies something more than the peaceful fruition of their philosophies and ideals matured by honest discussion and submitted to the ballot. It means some violent wrench in the whole philosophy of a people—a wrench from their ideas and ideals whence sprang their institutions and their form of government. In many democratic states it has meant the imposition of a new philosophy, changed ideas and changed ideals without their open submission to the people, and often without the people recognizing its approach until it had become a reality. And not a few of these recent revolutions have been stimulated by ambitious men preying upon the suffering of humanity for personal power.

An analysis of these foreign revolutions away from democracy reveals different sequences and methods in different countries, but they have a common pattern varying only in degree of violence of action. Their mild form is the breaking down of confidence in existing institutions by defamation, their violent form is overthrow of these institutions through seizure or suppression. They vary between initial winning of elections through promises not intended of fulfillment, and the direct "postponement" or abolition of elections. They gently secure the amiable surrender of the independence of legislative bodies by the delegation of their powers for "emergency sake" or else these bodies are harshly reorganized or adjourned. They encroach by evasion and subtle intimidation of judicial independence or they suppress the courts. In combating criticism their methods range between manipulation of the agencies of public information and the suppression of free speech and free press. These revolutions often enough continue old governmental forms for appearance's sake, but they all move forward to destruction of Liberty by the growth of disguised or open dictatorship.

None of the whole gamut of these new social ideas can be imposed without play upon fear or intimidation. They cannot be imposed nor can they be administered except through the harsh curbing of freedom, for some men always resist the reduction of their liberties.

THEIR EPILOGUE

Thus the scene of the tragedy of Liberty the world over must be suffering and discontent among the people. The drama moves swiftly in a torrent of words in which real purposes are disguised in portrayals of Utopia; idealism without realism; slogans, phrases and statements destructive to confidence in existing institutions; demands for violent action against slowly curable ills; unfair representation that sporadic wickedness is the system itself; searing prejudice against the former order; dismay and panic in the economic organization which feeds on its own despair. Emotions rise above reason. The man on horseback, ascending triumphantly to office on the steps of constitutional processes, demands and threatens the parliament into the delegation of its sacred power. Then follows consolidation of authority through powerful propaganda in the pay of the state to transform the mentality of the people. Resentment of criticism, denunciation of all oppositions, moral terrorization, all follow the sequence. The last scene is the suppression of freedom. Liberty dies of the water from her own well—free speech—poisoned by untruth.

In the Epilogue the dreams of those who saw Utopia are shattered and the people find they are marching backward toward the Middle Ages—as regimented men.

Chapter 2

Our American Heritage

ORIGIN OF OUR LIBERTIES

It may be tiresome to impatient spirits, but in view of the forces moving both abroad and at home which threaten freedom, every American may well spend a moment on the origins of his liberties, their development, their ideals, and their present vitality to solve our national problems.

The philosophy of Liberty had its beginnings when freedom of mind and spirit awoke from the Middle Ages in the Renaissance and the Reformation. It became positive in its expression through our English forebearers at Runnymede, in the enactment of the *habeas corpus*, and in provision for control of taxation by elected representatives of the people.

The migration of our forefathers to America was in refuge from the continued regimentation of men and men's minds still frozen by classes, by feudalism, by the churches, and by governments. Liberty was already implicit in their religious beliefs and their spiritual aspirations. Their purpose was to establish it in government. For the American Revolution was not alone a struggle for national independence. Our forefathers were equally insistent that they were fighting for a new liberty of men.

Their ideas were expressed currently, "that all men are created equal, that they are endowed by their Creator with certain unalienable Rights, that among these are Life, Liberty, and the pursuit of Happiness. That to secure these rights Governments are instituted among Men, deriving their just powers from the consent of the governed." And they shocked the world by denial of the Divine Right of Kings.

They refused to be satisfied with the Constitution until it more amply defined these unalienable rights than by the implications of its text. They introduced in the first amendments a concrete definition of the guarantees of liberty for the individual by declaring among other things that there should be no governmental or any other interference in the freedom of worship, of speech, of the press, of peaceable assembly, of petition, no invasion of the security of their persons, houses, papers, and effects against unreasonable searches and seizures, and then only by warrant of law.

They insisted that a person accused of crime should have the right of speedy and public trial by an impartial jury; that he should be informed of the charge; that he should have the right to call witnesses and be assisted by counsel; that he should not be compelled in any criminal case to bear witness against himself; that he should not be deprived of life, liberty, or property without due process of law, and that private property should not be taken for public use without just compensation.

Later in our history, after the Civil War, by further amendments these rights and immunities were reinforced by freedom from slavery and by still further guarantees of equality before the law and in franchise. Later, by amendment, the franchise was extended to women. Thus our system is built not only upon declared rights and securities but upon an equality of these rights to all.

THE METHOD OF THEIR ESTABLISHMENT

In the field of government, the fathers, as the consequence of the philosophy of Liberty, devised a mechanism of self-government under a charter of fundamental law designed for the sole purpose of protecting and defending this freedom. Our Federal Constitution was based upon the conception that the safeguard of free men rested upon explicit law; and that the law should spring from the expressed will of the majority of the people themselves. The unique feature of its framework was the independence of the executive, legislative, and judicial powers, the checks and balances between State and Federal authority which should guarantee and sustain these rights and liberties "to the end that it may be a government of laws and not of men.[2] They set up machinery for its amendment that would require time to stop, look, and listen in order that transient emotions might cool, in the expectation that, recalling its transcendent purpose, the people should be slow to abrogate their liberties.

THE PURPOSE

The purpose, the hope, and the prayer of the Founders of the Republic was "to form a more perfect Union, establish Justice, insure domestic Tranquility, provide for the common defense, promote the general Welfare and secure the Blessings of Liberty to ourselves and our posterity." They

[2]As expressed in the Massachusetts Constitution.

reinforced our frame of government by dual responsibility; on the one hand, through the Federal Government to maintain our freedom among nations, and with its immense resources and power to protect our people in the event of failure of local government from internal suffering or disorder. On the other hand,, under guarantees from the Federal Government, the States were to preserve individual liberty through the responsibilities of local self-government.Thus our American Republic was the first of the modern nations to place into the structure of government the whole social philosophy of Liberty, with its care for the worth and integrity of the individual, with its security of unalienable human rights. Thereby came the emancipation of the lives and minds of American men and women into the mastery of their own destinies, for they were the masters of men. Thereby they gave the light of freedom to the whole New World and a workable system of government for its protection. Our fathers died willingly that we might come into this, the most stupendous inheritance men could bequeath to a race.

Chapter 3

The Utility and Ideals of Liberty

Ever since the woof of our form of government was woven into the warp of Liberty at the Revolution, we have been unceasing in our development of that Liberty until we have made an American System, rooted into our soil, ingrained into our lives. It differs in important ways from all the liberal systems, of Europe. Therefore, I do not speak of British Liberalism, or French Liberalism. I do not speak of the Liberalism of the eighteenth century or the early Victorians. I speak of American Liberalism. It has always been a living creed, advancing to meet the problems of our particular world.

THE GROWTH OF AMERICAN LIBERTY

True American Liberalism is not a system of frozen procedures; its very nature is progressive, for its own processes stimulate growth. From the very stimulus which freedom gives to man we have created great problems rising from our expansion over a continent, from a forty times multiplied population, from the development of a huge industry and commerce from defensive war. And growth and changing scenes necessitate growth in the methods of protection to liberty.

ITS CONSTANT REFORM OF PROTECTIONS

Constant reform is an essential part of its process, not alone to sweep up the ever recurring tendency of strong groups to consolidate privilege, and of citizens to surrender their liberties for economic gains or hopes, but more importantly, because advancing thought, science, discovery, and invention are constantly imposing new surroundings upon us. Yet, until recently, in all of our continuous adjustments we have preserved the great individual rights with which men were endowed by the Creator. Nor have we receded from the Constitutional principle that not even government shall trespass upon them.

Our American System has ever recognized that the borders between liberty and license, between free speech and slander, order and disorder, enterprise and exploitation, private interest and public interest are difficult to define. But the domain of liberty can be defined by virtue, reason, by the common will, and by law. It cannot be defined by arbitrary power.

ITS FOUNDATIONS IN BIOLOGY AND UTILITY

American Liberty, through its enthronement of the individual, has proved over generations to have deep roots both in utility and in human experience. We must examine here some very practical questions, for upon them hinge great issues.

Any society to be successful must secure the effort and initiative of its citizens. Otherwise it will stagnate or degenerate. To meet its needs and to advance its civilization it must encourage the impulses which motivate the individual to action and achievement. Therefore any workable philosophy of society or framework of government must take account of the raw materials of human nature, from which its motivations or human drives arise, if it would build for the betterment of the nation.

CHARACTERISTICS OF HUMAN BEHAVIOR

If we examine the characteristics of human nature and human behavior we find they are mostly born in man and change but slowly. Without attempting to determine relative importance, we find that they comprise certain hereditary human instincts and certain acquired desires.

There are such evil instincts and impulses as shiftlessness, envy, hate, malice, fear, overpugnacity, greed, and will to destruction. These require no discussion except in terms of repression.

There are the selfish instincts and impulses of self-preservation, acquisitiveness, curiosity, rivalry, ambition, desire for self-expression, for adulation, for power.

There are altruistic instincts of courage, love and fealty to family and to country; of pity, of kindness and generosity; of love of liberty and of justice; the desire to work and construct, for expression of creative faculties; the impulse to serve the community and nation; and with these also hope, faith, and the mystical yearnings for spiritual things.

All these instincts and qualities vary in proportion in every individual and their proportions are modified by intelligence, ability and physical vigor. They are further modified by education, by moral and spiritual training, by the vast fund of human experience, and the vast plant and equipment of civilization which we pass on with increments to each succeeding generation. From these instincts, impulses, desires, and characteristics come drive to action, initiative, leadership; production of hand and mind;

cooperation; the highest development of thought and spirituality. From them come not alone the forces of progress but also the injuries to freedom which range through oppression, crime, and injustice.

But whatever their division among us, one thing can be stated in finality. Instinct, character, and the divine spark in the human soul are the property alone of the individual. There can be no human thought, no impulse to action, which does not arise from the individual. A free people maintains as many potential centers of enterprise, leadership, and intellectual and spiritual progress as there are individuals. We might as well talk of abolishing the sun's rays if we would secure our food, as to talk of abolishing individualism as a basis of successful society.

OUR ECONOMIC SYSTEM

Economic laws may be said to be the deduction from human experience of the average response of these varied selfish or altruistic raw materials of the human animal when applied in the mass. These cannot be repealed by official fiat. It is precisely upon this rock of human behavior that the most perfect academic hopes and panaceas are wrecked. Those amateur sociologists who are misleading this nation by ignoring the biological foundations of human action are as far from common sense as an engineer who ignored physics in bridge building. No economic equality can survive the working of biological inequality. This is a hard commonplace truth, disappointing as it may be to those who ride upon the plans of Utopia. For at least the next generations we dare not wholly abandon self-interest as a component of motive forces to initiative, to enterprise, to leadership.

Out of these complex and powerful instincts and impulses human experience over generations has developed an economic system which we may define as one of private property, competitive production and distribution of goods and services in hope of a profit, the payment of differential wages and salaries based upon abilities and services, the savings of earnings and profits, the lending of them at interest through their investment in our productive plant.

This system of rewards to stimulate the creative instincts and impulses which motivate men secured the application of all their infinitely varied energies. Therefrom comes the transformation of the products of nature and their distribution as the goods and services which provide for the nation. It also secures the self-denial, thrift, and savings of a multitude of people which provide the productive capital from which we build our tools and equipment.

Through competition we secure the most potent stimulant to improvement and progress. The manager's restless pillow has done more to advance the practical arts than all the legislation upon the statute books. Competition curbs rapacity and attempts at economic domination. Ours is a system of losses to the least intelligent producers as well as profits to the more intelligent, and while some individuals may at times profit unduly or may abuse Liberty, in the end it is the consumer that wins through the production of the plenty of goods and services. For he is the beneficiary of that increasing production at constantly lower costs which we require to reach our social objective—in constantly increasing standards of living. This system is greatly modified from the ray by the increasing knowledge of what constitutes self-interest, but more importantly by the ideals and standards vital to secure ordered liberty.

It has in many ways become uniquely American. From unprecedented invention and method we have developed low unit costs by mass production and by large scale operation. Mass production rests necessarily upon great accumulations of capital from a multitude of savings and it succeeds by arousing mass desire and mass consumption. In turn this can be reached only by low unit profit and increasing purchasing power through higher real wages and salaries.

LEADERSHIP

Overriding all economic details, it is certain that any hope of conducting this vast complex of civilization and of assuring progress for the future must lie in the development of millions of individuals for leadership in every agency of life, great or small. Leadership cannot be discovered by birth, nor bred like queen bees, nor assured by the appointment of autocrats or bureaucrats. This immense necessity of society can be supplied only from a full recruiting, out of the whole mass of the people, through the sifting test of competition among free men and women. If there were no other reason, this is the justification of the competitive system, for without its constant renewal of leadership our increasingly complex civilization will cease properly to function. Moreover, in a broad way, the only individuals who can successfully conduct these millions of organizations which we have created to carry on our daily life are those who have a self-interest in the results from them and have risen to leadership in them by their own worth.

THE IDEALS OF LIBERTY

No civilization could be built to endure solely upon a groundwork of greed or even upon the enlightened self-interest of the individual. It is out of the altruistic and constructive impulses that the standards and the ideals of the nation are molded and sustained.

Our American System is not alone an economic method, a definition of rights, a scheme of representative government, an organization to maintain order and justice, a release of constructive instincts and desires. It is far more than that, for it is a system of stimulation to higher standards, to higher aspirations and ideals.

While we have built a gigantic organized society upon the attainment of the individual, we should not have raised a brick of it but by the stimulation of self-restraint and by drawing upon those high aspirations of men and women expressed in their standards of truth and justice and in their spiritual yearnings.

These ideals are never wholly realized. Not a single human being personifies their complete realization. It is therefore not surprising that society, a collection of persons, a necessary maze of instincts of individuals, cannot realize its ideals wholly.

We may examine what some of these ideals are. The first concern of the American System is for spiritual health and growth of men. It does not accept that the end and object of civilization or the pursuit of happiness lies in being well-fed or growing fat. It denies the economic concept of history, or that blind materialism can long engage the loyalties of mankind. Its faith is that the divine spark, the ideals, the conscience, the courage, the patriotism, the heroism, and the humanism of men make human destiny. It holds that freedom is a prize to be sought for itself, for from it come the infinite satisfactions of the spirit, far more important than all the goods and gadgets of life.

American Liberalism holds that moral and spiritual advancement among men can come only through the freedom of individual conscience and opinion, and the responsibilities which of themselves come only in freedom. The very basis of freedom is justice, and our philosophy holds that justice extends further than protection of legal rights; that it extends into those fields of social elations which are outside the law; that every individual shall be given a fair chance—an equality of opportunity. It holds that there should be a just diffusion of national income which will give protection and security to those who have the will to work.

American Liberty denies that special privileges come to men by birth; it denies the whole concept of frozen class and of class conflict, for these stratifications are barriers to the free spirit and the free rise of the individual by his own effort.

The humanism of our system demands the protection of the suffering and the unfortunate. It places that prime responsibility upon the individual for the welfare of his neighbor, but it insists also that in necessity the local community, the State government, and in the last resort, the National government shall give protection to them. But it also insists that the full exercise of this responsibility by every individual and institution is an essential of sustained Liberty.

It holds that the very sustenance of Liberty and the hope of humanity is in cooperation. It holds that this cooperation may be promoted by government, but to Liberty cooperation is a concept of consent among free men, not the compulsion of regimented men.

It holds that the other freedoms cannot be maintained if economic freedom be impaired—not alone because the most insidious mastery of men's minds and lives is through economic domination, but because the maximum possible economic freedom is the most nearly universal field for release of the creative spirit of men. Therefore, in fashioning its economic system, it does not hold that there is a license of business to exploit; on the contrary, it holds that economic oppression is servitude. The American System holds equally that monopoly, group or class advantage, economic domination, Regimentation, Fascism, Socialism, Communism, or any other form of tyranny, small or great, are violations of the basis of Liberty.

True Liberty requires that all claims to human power must be subject to live criticism and common judgment. The primary protections of humanity from oppressions either by private action or by government are the liberties of expression and protest. Ours is the sole system which maintains within itself the forces of corrective antagonism to oppression of any kind whether they come from the "right" or the "left."

We may justifiably say that our system builded on Liberty stimulates those constructive instincts and aspirations through which men and women develop their individual capabilities to the maximum achievement; and that the sum of such achievements is far greater than that possible under any other system which stultifies these desires and aspirations. Its essence is justice, self-restraint, obligation to fellow men. Its practice is a sensitive adjustment of conflicting rights and interests through a spirit of decency and co-operation in human relationships, reinforced by governmental restraints, to the end that men may enjoy equal opportunities. It has proved the broadest road and the surest to human progress.

Hardly twenty years ago we accepted our liberties as we accepted the air we breathed. We burned incense to those forefathers who died to win them for us and to those who devised a government which assured them to us. We were so confident of the rightness of our ideals and our institutions that we would "make the world safe for democracy." No man thought they lay endangered within his lifetime. Yet today men freely debate how much of these we will surrender.

Chapter 4

The Accomplishments of the American System

APPRAISAL OF OUR ACCOMPLISHMENT

Signor Mussolini states: "Today the Liberal faith must shut the doors of its deserted temples, deserted because the peoples of the world realize that its worship—agnostic in the field of economics and indifferent in the field of politics and morals—will lead as it has already led to certain ruin." We have many voices at home who are likewise informing us that we must change to some other faith.

Before we depart from American Liberty and plunge into the alternatives urged upon us, we should pause to examine not only the character of its foundations, but its record of attainments, and the degree of its "ruin." We must do this, although to mention accomplishments of the American System is in these days a perilous adventure, since little of it can be admitted and at the same time justify much of the current oratory. But there does remain a vast majority of our people who are proud of our race, the great epic of its accomplishment and its stirring spiritual forces of progress.

The strength of a social system for the betterment of humanity is to be measured not alone by its ideals, and by its practicability, but by its comparison with others and even more by its record of achievement. It is not to be measured by the arraignment of human weaknesses on its margins or by contrast with perfection, as valuable as the dreams of beatitude truly are. And any appraisal of accomplishment concerns not material progress alone. More importantly, it comprises intellectual, moral, spiritual, and social advancement.

We need go back scarcely more than a single generation in this examination, and indeed, it is the last generation in national life that is the important period of test, for it is over the last generation and not previous generations nor a single year or five years, that the movement toward present decadence or progress becomes evident.

CONTRAST WITH OTHER NATIONS

For many years in practice of my profession and in public service I journeyed to other countries. My occupation was not as a tourist but as one engaged intimately with those peoples, associated in their daily lives and problems, in contact with their social systems, their governments, their thoughts, their hopes and their progress. In England, in Germany, in France, in Italy, in Russia, in China, in India, in Latin America, and in Australia alike, the great mass of people viewed the progress and the liberty of America as an ideal. And to me every homecoming was an inspiration. I found again a greater kindness, a greater neighborliness, a greater sense of individual responsibility, a lesser poverty, a greater comfort and security of our people, a wider spread of education a wider diffusion of the finer arts and appreciation of them, a greater freedom of spirit, a wider opportunity for our children, and higher hopes of the future, than in any other country in the world.

SECURITY

The American System has gone further toward solutions of economic security of the individual than any other system of society. Our diffusion of national income has its faults, but even English Liberalism has today double the proportion of the people under the real poverty line that we have. Fascism has made improvement in Italy, but at an immeasurable cost of human liberty, and its attainments are far below what the American System had already accomplished. And we stand in brilliant contrast with the drab failure of the Socialist system of production as we see it at work in its great Socialist exemplar, Russia.

EDUCATION, SCIENCE, HUMAN JUSTICE

Statistics indicate only the bones of the social body but they do indicate its strength. If we were to compare the proportions in each thousand of our population with those of the most advanced nation of Europe, we would find some reassuring evidences of our strength. We have a third more of our children a longer time in primary schools than has that country. We have proportionally three times as many in secondary schools, we have over six times as many in institutions of higher learning.

We have a far wider diffusion among the people of books, magazines, and newspapers than any other country. In proportion to our numbers we have developed ten times as many laboratories of scientific research and invention. Our application of scientific discovery has grown at a pace far beyond that of any other nation. While it has increased our problems, yet with the increased productivity from it has come the enlargement of leisure and the extension of constructive recreation. We have come into a fuller life for all of the people, have given increasing scope to creative power and the expansion of every man's mind.

More than any other leading country we had advanced the realities of human justice—not alone in education but in a vast series of protections to children, to public health, to conditions of labor, and by regulations of business activities—making firm the open door of opportunity.

HUMAN CARE, COOPERATION, WORKING RELATIONSHIPS

The humanness of our people and our sense of community responsibility had grown steadily. During the past generation we had more nearly met with a full hand a most sacred obligation of man, the responsibility of a man to his neighbor. Support to our schools, hospitals, and institutions for the care of the afflicted had surpassed in totals of billions the service in any period of history proportionate to any other nation in the world. Our provisions, through community, local, state, and national government, for hospitalization, for care of those who had met misfortune, our care of orphans, the aged, the victims of storm, flood and drought, were nearing the full need. No finer spirit of a people can be found than has been shown by ours in the universe and untiring support of those in distress from the depression.

We have gained enormously in the sense and method of cooperation and its moving spirit has had no parallel in any other race. Tens of thousands of associations meet in village and city for the advancement of economic, scientific, moral and social, professional and governmental ideas. Through their exchange of ideas, their coordination of action, their lift in standards and ideals, we had greatly developed in the highest area of government—that is, self-government outside of formal government.

Industry had made strides in understanding its public obligations and progress in the sense of trusteeship involved in the conduct of corporate life. That understanding has been on average higher than those of other peoples. We have heart-breaking violations, but we demand higher standards than other nations and we get more irritated and vocal when our standards are not met. Until lately there was profound improvement in the relation of the employer and the employed. Organized labor had won great advances. As a nation we had accepted the principle of collective bargaining and that the courts must not be used in its prevention. We had embraced the thesis that payment of the highest real wage was the most effective way to increased economic and social progress, and that industry had a definite obligation to its employees outside of their wage. Labor had in the main rejected the foreign formulas of limitation of effort. The hours of labor had decreased successively, and the twelve-hour, the eleven-hour, the ten-hour, and nine-hour day had disappeared. Child labor had decreased by over two-thirds in the twenty years before 1930.

Our System of Liberty—through its stimulation of competitive individual effort, its creation of enterprise, its development of skill, and its discoveries in science and invention which come from intellectual freedom—had secured the production of the greatest quantities of commodities and services and in the most infinite variety known in the history of man. We can say without qualification that the motivation of production based on private initiative had proved the very mother of plenty. Thus the outstanding accomplishment of our economic system was that for the first time in the history of the world and almost alone among nations we produced not only plenty[3] to supply the minimum needs of our whole population for food, clothing, shelter, the protections of government, intellectual development, and recreation, but a larger measure of comforts.

OUR ATTAINMENT OF A "PLENTY"

The triumph of our degree of economy of plenty over an economy of scarcity represents the highest economic achievement of civilization. It has had visible demonstration in this last generation. In this short period of one generation, and even before the recent boom, the number of our families, and therefore our homes, had increased by 9,000,000. In that time we had builded for them 15,000,000 new and better homes. In proportion to each hundred thousand of our people we had equipped four times as many homes with electricity as any other great nation; thereby we lifted infinite drudgery from women and men.

The barriers of time and space had been swept away. Life had been made freer, the intellectual vision of every individual had been expanded, by bringing to them, in proportion to our numbers, four times as many telephones, five times as many radios, and six times as many automobiles as any great nation of Europe. Our cities had been made magnificent with beautiful buildings, parks, and playgrounds. Our countryside had been knit together with

[3]I prefer the term "plenty" rather than a "surplus." as the latter term becomes confused with isolated and temporary overproduction. The "economy of scarcity" attributed to our system by some economists seems to be a play on words or a denial of obvious facts. Mr Henry Ford hardly bases his operations upon creating a scarcity.

splendid roads. We had increased by twelve times the use of electric power in industry and thereby taken the sweat from the backs of men. In this great climb real wages and the purchasing power of men and women had steadily increased over the generation.

Socially and despite all the theorists, we were steadily lessening any tendency of our people toward social and economic class stratification until the recent stimulation of class feeling. If the Socialists, Communists, and other collectivists would but compute the farm and home owners, the individual small business people, the insurance policy holders, the savings bank depositors, the small investors, the stockholders, and the employees of secured position and future, they would find us without that dimension of "proletariat" upon which all their appeals to hate are based. By that term is meant the group in poverty without hope for the betterment of their children. Outside of the transitory paralysis of the Great Depression, that group has steadily decreased.

IMPROVEMENT IN GOVERNMENT

In the field of government I believe that any careful student will agree that during this generation the efficiency and integrity of public administration, whether national, state, or municipal, had sensibly improved despite some bad exhibits. Our unique American national habit of washing our dirty government linen in public, a habit itself an indication of moral virility, tends to obscure the fact that even our weakest spot in government, the municipalities, had markedly improved over a generation.

This showing of a single American generation, after many other generations of steady improvement in human living, this advance of comfort and intellectual life, inspiration and ideals, did not arise without right principles animating the American System which produced them.

But above all other accomplishments our system was constant in asserting the rights of men against government and domestic tyranny, for ours was a vigorous and vocal opponent of human wrongs. Outstanding, undimmed and challenging, it was the hope of opportunity and freedom for men and women.

THE DEPRESSION

Five years ago there came the earthquake of world-wide depression from world-wide causes. Businessmen and farmers suffered bitter distress. Three or four million families lost the earnings of their breadwinners, poverty stalked in the land as we had not known it since the like aftermath of the Civil War.

In the view of the character of the storm, the nation may thank God that twenty-one millions of families still had their living. It is one of the greatest testimonies of the staunchness of the structure of American Liberty that immediately upon this disaster the country was organized and giving unfailing food and shelter to those in distress, supplied through the idealism of the nation which accepted its responsibilities and through the sacrifice of those who were kept at work. Manfully the nation was adjusting the strains of the depression and was accomplishing it without strikes and without social clash.

And it might be observed through it all that the structure which was builded over these years was not so much in "ruins" that it did not produce more goods than bureaucracy could tolerate, that some 30,000,000 children continued to attend school in the "ruins;" that millions of people continued to find spiritual inspiration in churches still standing in the "ruins;" that other millions daily attended games, theatres, and recreations in the "ruins;" and that 23,000,000 automobiles were running about in our "ruins" at ever increasing speeds.

ABUSES OF LIBERTY

The depression brought vividly to the surface many failures in American life, many weaknesses latent in the organization of the system, many wickednesses and abuses of Liberty. Some of them are far deeper than the depression. We witnessed tragedy after tragedy to American aspirations and ideals. Abuses of Liberty through betrayal of trust or through economic domination, whether they be called "unfair competition," special privilege, monopoly, exploitation, vicious speculation, or the use of property to oppress others, are all sins against the whole system and ideals of Liberty. Thoughtful men had long warned of these weaknesses, but the American people are slow to move by an abstraction. Here indeed has been the battleground of Liberty against oppression ever since the beginning of the Industrial Age. Upon our conceptions of duty, our courage, and our abilities will Liberty survive.

In the confusion of striving to overcome the depression, and the multitude of social and economic problems born of our progress and a wider vision of human betterment, the American System of Liberty has been challenged and the cry has gone up that these problems be solved within a frame of government which cannot itself infringe upon Liberty. Here is indeed the real test.

I shall deal later with the vitality and the capacity of the true American System to overcome these dangers, but before doing so I shall discuss the alternative systems which are offered to us. For "eternal vigilance" is today not alone a fight against the growth of economic oppression within our walls but the invasion of these other systems from without.

The American people have been greatly discouraged these last four years and in the presence of immediate difficulties have sometimes forgotten the grandeur of our accomplishments, the genius of our people, and the future promise of our national life.

Our present difficulties—great as they are—do not justify the assumption that a system of life builded on such sacrifice over a century and a half with such a record of achievement should be discarded or crippled, or that the philosophy of Liberty is all wrong, or even that we "must sacrifice some of our liberties." For this period is no more typical of the American System than all the other aftermaths of war in the previous century or than all the other bubbles of crazy inflation in history.

It is not as if this were a mere machine that we are contemplating—for, mind you, in America we are dealing with one of the last few strongholds of human freedom. Its liberties did not come to us as a gift—they were bought by the blood of men who fought for them.

Chapter 5

Alternative Philosophies of Society and Government

We may briefly examine the other social philosophies which are today offered as a challenge to our American System. Those which rise to importance in discussion are Socialism, Communism, Fascism, Naziism, and National Regimentation. They all have in common the idea of the servitude of the individual to the state, and the denial of liberties unassailable by the state.

OLDER PHILOSOPHIES

There are other systems which have arisen in the past, theocracy, patriarchy, oligarchy, autocracy, despotism, monarchy, feudalism. They likewise held to this common idea that men are the servants and pawns of the state, and most of them sheltered their omnipotence over human rights in the claim of Divine Right. Some of these old systems still linger in places in the world, but they have no present importance to us except as laboratory records of human experience.

RECENT PHILOSOPHIES

It is rather a remarkable fact that while the alternative systems of society which are proposed to us have organized exponents who expound their philosophy, their ideals, their patterns, their methods, their promised, and their superiorities, we have little definite exposition of the philosophy, purpose, attainments, and the objectives of true American Liberalism.

DIFFICULTIES OF DEFINITION

A primary difficulty in any discussion of social philosophies is a definition of words and terms. They are not often defined alike by friends and foes or even among friends. That is perhaps natural, for each contains many ideas and consequences which can be given different weights in expounding their ideologies. There is also a large element of "slogan" and opprobrium in their use. The exponents of each assign most of the beatitudes to their system and all the failures of humanity to the others. We may, however, so far as they are available, adopt the definitions of proponents.

LAISSEZ FAIRE

Before I proceed to discuss these alternate philosophies of society and government I shall, in order to clear some underbrush, take a moment to discuss one of the older economic systems, the ghost of which seems to walk the minds of some of our contemporary essayists. That is *laissez faire*.

This old economic theory of the French Physiocrats of the eighteenth century and of its exponent in modified form, Adam Smith, has been lately revived as a vivid slogan, mostly for political defamation. It is the theory of economic "let do," "go as you please," or "let nature rule," and is defined in academic terms as, "The doctrine that the business man should be allowed to go his own way while the government's only duty is to give him protection and perform a few general services, preserve peace, and punish crime." This was originally thought to be the essential component of all forms of individualism. It may thrive as an economic or social philosophy in some country areas today, but it has been dead in America for generations—except in books on economic history. It is now, however, trotted out and forms a comforting political invective for use by a long list of collectivist writers who infer that it dominated and directed the policies of the United States up to some recent date, when it was suddenly vanquished—and abandoned.

Another term associated by some with *laissez faire* is "Capitalism." This again is a term of indefinite meaning depending upon who uses it. It is employed by the enemies of the American system for purposes of slur.

The American economic system is hardly one of "let do" or "go as you please." Ever since the Industrial Age began we have devised and enforced thousands of regulations in prevention of economic domination or abuse of our liberties through the growing instruments of business. Furthermore, the sense of public responsibility for the general welfare has successively produced public education, public health, public works, public stimulation of scientific research, and in 1929 for the first time embraced the responsibility for public action in the battle against depression. This is hardly *laissez faire*.

If our economic system was abandoned at some recent date, as some persons purport, then we must face the only alternatives—the consequences of one or the others of Regimentation, Fascism, Socialism or Communism. If its marginal weaknesses are to be reformed, as they constantly must be, then that is neither revolution, nor abandonment.

Some twelve years ago in the essay referred to before I expressed this view:

> Individualism cannot be maintained as the foundation of a society if it looks to only legalistic justice based upon contracts, property, and political equality. Such legalistic safeguards are themselves not enough. In our individualism we have long since abandoned the *laissez faire* of the 18th Century—the notion that it is "every man for himself and the devil take the hindmost." We abandoned that when we adopted the ideal of equality of opportunity—the fair chance of Abraham Lincoln. We have confirmed its abandonment in terms of legislation, of social and economic justice,—in part because we have learned that the foremost are not always the best nor the hindmost the worst—and in part because we have learned that social injustice is the destruction of justice itself. We have learned that the impulse to production can only be maintained at high pitch if there is a fair division of the product. We have also learned that fair division can only be obtained by certain restrictions on the strong and the dominant.

I have not, in the period of twelve years since, heard this idea disputed by any economist, sociologist, business man, politician, or statesman. There may be some reactionary souls who still yearn for *laissez faire*. But the lack of objection to the above statement might indicate that it has no passionate party in its support. It had passed out of living and thought but has since been reborn in the past twelve months only as a dishonest polemic, as a straw man, set up to be knocked down.

Every decent American and every sincere defender of the accomplishments of our people and the inherent soundness of their character and beliefs resents the charge that every wickedness in high place is because of our devotion to *laissez faire*. These horrid examples quoted to us daily are mostly violations of simple honesty or actions through the loopholes of law and the Ten Commandments and are not the bases of our economic or social system. If they were we should have perished some generations ago.

RUGGED INDIVIDUALISM

While discussing defamation of economic or social ideas, I might also spend a few lines upon the term "rugged individualism." This term is lately clothed in false habiliments of heartless disregard of public welfare and daily demolished by hot invective. Yet to maintain the varied individuality and personality of men and women is one of the assurances of progress. We have predicated our entire educational system and our entire social advancement upon the development of the special qualities of individualism, their personality and character. While I can make no claim for having introduced the term "rugged individualism," I should be proud to have invented it. It has been used by American leaders for over a half-century in eulogy of those God-fearing men and women of honesty whose stamina and character and fearless assertion of rights led them to make their own way in life. It is they who have borne the burdens and given leadership in their communities. Rugged individualism is indeed a distinguishing and enduring quality ever found in Americans. It gives lifeblood to such basic principles as freedom of speech, conscience, press, and equality before the law, regardless of race or religion. It contributes to the saving of our souls and character "from the deadening pressure of conformity and false ideals."

SOCIALISM

Socialism has many definitions. One authoritative statement of it is as follows:

The chief principles of Socialism may perhaps be reduced to these:

1. The abolition of the rights of private ownership in the means of production (natural resources and capital) with retention of private property in articles of personal use; this implies state ownership of the means of production.

2. The administration of the means of production collectively by the state through a democratic political organization.

3. The abolition of the wage system as it is at present constituted; and the substitution for ours of another scheme for the apportionment of income.[4]

The long-time slogan of the British Socialists was "Government ownership and operation of all the agencies of production, distribution and exchange."

Other less frank groups, parading the cloak of Liberalism, take variously milder positions advocating government ownership and operation of less extensive economic areas, and by the moderation of their demands some of them honestly do not believe themselves to be, and would even deny they are, Socialists.

Except for Communists, few of the modern Socialists advocate violence, but seek to attain their goal by working through the established agencies of government, thus gradually pushing the nation into their path, inch by inch. They realize that any step taken by government into ownership and operation of no matter how small a segment of an industry will be followed rapidly by other steps. For they know that, through the insatiable appetite of bureaucracy to enlarge itself, and the ability of government to disorganize the

[4]*American Economic Life*, Tugwell, Munroe, and Stryker (New York: Harcourt Brace, 1930), p. 685.

adequate service of competing private enterprise, there will grow apparent justification for the spread of the Socialist system. They anticipate also that the owners of private enterprise, trying to compete with such tyranny in government (for which the taxpayer stands the losses), will often enough in despair become willing or even anxious to join in advocating government purchase to protect their savings. This is probably true. The greatest chance of Socialism is not the agitation of immature academic minds, nor the violent Communists. It is that even a moderate adoption of government operation will so destroy confidence and so drive the economic system into disorganization that the harassed business men, desiring to save something, will align themselves in advocating government purchase, or that in face of chaos the people will turn more and more to economic "action."

True American Liberalism utterly denies the whole creed of Socialism. The disguised or open objective of Socialism is equality of income, wages or economic rewards. The tenet of equality in true Liberalism is a tenet of equality in birth, equality before the law, and equality of opportunity as distinguished from equality of reward for services. True Liberalism insists that to equalize rewards and possession of material things robs the individual of free imagination, inventiveness, risk, adventure, and individual attainment, development of personality, and independence from a monotony that would sentence the soul to imprisonment. It denies the Socialist contention that men will be more free when compelled to work under, and to work for, only one employer—the government.

It is important here to repeat that Liberty denies that the materials of life adequate to meet the needs of society can be obtained without reward proportionate to ability and service. It rejects the theory that men will strive to the utmost and will deny themselves from enjoying immediately the whole of the daily income unless they have confidence in the protection of their honestly acquired savings, and thus may protect themselves and their children by their own means and possessions against a rainy day. It holds that ample leadership and improvement cannot be found under the bushel of government bureaucracy. It denies that politicians can manage the economic system as well as the people who have risen in it and whose hopes and security of living rest in advancing it. The American System can point not only to theory but to practice. We have already seen our government try to operate railroads and ships. We know the results. The Socialists are fond of eulogizing the post office as a great example of successful Socialism. That the government should control the mails for reasons of confidence is not denied, but that private enterprise could collect and deliver the mail for three-quarters of the present cost is obvious to anyone competent to study the subject. One thing is a certainty: that if all industry, through the inescapable play of political bureaucratic action, were reduced to the efficiency of the post office, we should fail within a few years to produce sufficient to feed, clothe, and care for our people.

These arguments are limited to the workability and utility of the Socialist system. There is a much larger aspect. The Socialists claim they would maintain democratic institutions and all other freedoms except economic freedom. Democratic institutions would not last long. Producing economic equality by regimenting of the whole population into government employees scarcely assures the election of an independent legislative body or any other independent official. Nor can such administration be conducted during the existence of legislative bodies, with all their inevitable interferences, with all their necessary sectionalism, party criticism, and their perennial pull and haul for advancement of individual constituents. Legislative bodies cannot exist if they delegate their authority to any dictator, but without such delegation every member of these bodies in such a scene is impelled by the interest of his constituents constantly to seek privilege and to interfere in the administering of economic agencies.

For Socialism to maintain its hold against those who still aspire to liberty every guaranty of freedom—free speech, free press, assembly or a free legislative body, a free judiciary—ultimately must be suppressed. In order to give Socialism a fighting chance the whole structure of our government—constitution, courts, legislative and executive arms—must first be merged under despotism. While I shall deal with these effects more fully later on, I may mention here that the attempt to foist Socialism onto democratic institutions was a large part of the cause of the collapse of these institutions in Italy, Germany, Austria, Poland, and in other places, with the inevitable leap of dictatorship to their place.

And I may add a word to that group of people in and out of government who are playing with Socialist fire without expecting it really to burn. The penetration of Socialist methods even to a partial degree will demoralize the economic system, the legislative bodies, and in fact the whole system of ordered Liberty. No people for long will permit demoralization. In the United States the reaction from such chaos will not be more Socialism but will be toward Fascism. That inevitably is not only establishable from internal study of the forces in the United States but it has been the invariable turn in foreign countries where there is a considerable economic middle class. And this group is proportionately larger in the United States than in any other country in the world. The path of Socialism leads straight to its own downfall together with the pillars of Liberty.

COMMUNISM

Communism is merely the imposition of Socialism all at once by violence, and Bolshevism is the insistence that the Proletariat shall administer such imposition. It is difficult to find positive definitions of Communism among its friends. They are mostly involved in polemics against other systems. A few partial definitions are:

> The basis of Communist society must be the social ownership of the means of production and exchange.[5]

> Communists everywhere support every revolutionary movement against extant social and political conditions.[6]

> Bolshevism is the revolutionary, Marxist movement in the Russian and international labor movement...[7]

Fortunately or unfortunately for the world, we are able to observe Communism—that is Socialism—in its full form at work in a whole nation. With seventeen years of record in Russia we are no longer dependent upon combating a theory of Utopia. We can see it in practice. One of the favorite phrases and constant preoccupations of Communism is "Economic Planning." As to the results of this practical

---

[5]Bukharin, *The ABC of Communism* Communist Party of Great Britain, London, 1922, p. 70.

[6]Engels, *The Communist Manifesto*, International Publishers, New York, 1930, p.319 and p. 68.

[7]*Small Soviet Encyclopaedia*, Moscow, Vol. 1, p.791.

Socialism in action I may well quote an able social observer, who states his prior open-mindedness toward this experiment.[8]

> Surely the time has come for the intellectuals, the liberals and the radicals of the world to speak out about this new slavery, to call it clearly and bluntly what it is. For it can no longer be doubted that in this dictatorship of politicians is to be found every abuse which liberals and radicals have denounced in their own societies for generations...the Soviet has allowed its people to starve by the thousands.... It has choked all competition, and made itself a monopoly of monopolies; it has restored serfdom, conscription of labor, and indentured servitude among a people that had recently liberated itself by revolution and civil war, from these feudal chains;...it has kept wages low and labor intense, and has made democracy in the factory only a sham; it has herded and regimented its people like cattle. It has pitilessly industrialized its women under the pretense of emancipating them; it has crowded the population into dingy quarters, and offered every discouragement to the creation of homes.... It has stifled the growth of democracy, and has centralized power into a dictatorship of fanatics and machines; it has waged a class war against peasants, tradesmen, and metal workers;...there is no opportunity for the expression of the public will;...it has oppressed with unsurpassed barbarity men and women guilty of no other crime than the prosperity attendant upon enterprise, industry, intelligence, and thrift; it has refused the rights of *habeas corpus*, of trial by jury, of equality before the law; it has sent its secret police into a million homes;...it has terrorized the public with marching armies, secret police, merciless penalties, and a million spies. It has deported or shot hundreds of thousands of men and women solely for political heresy and non-conformance.... It has suppressed all freedom of speech or assembly, and in effect has raised a thousand obstacles against the freedom of worship and belief... Slavery, barbarism and desolation—these fundamentally, despite a thousand minor virtues, is what Russia is today.

[8]Will Durant, *The Tragedy of Russia,* Simon and Schuster, pp. 150-54.

Here we see applied Socialism in a country larger and even more varied in its natural resources than the United States, where by extinguishing all self-interest and all freedom it has not been able to secure enough production to feed its people. The standard of living to the whole population (except the officials and soldiers) is much lower than that of our people who are today on relief. Liberty is dead.

Whatever the maladjustments in the American System may be, it has been the very mother of plenty in production. It seems therefore inadvisable to adopt systems which although they promise equality in distribution fail to produce the commodities to distribute. But the other evils of Communism are far greater than the material ones. Freedom of men's minds and souls is more precious to the future of humanity than even the jam on their bread—which neither Socialism nor Communism will produce.

FASCISM

This theory rose to power under Premier Mussolini in the economic depression of 1922 when the Italian State was not only suffering from the post-war world-wide economic dislocation, but its dislocation was being greatly increased by Socialist and Communist activities.

Immediately upon Signor Mussolini's appointment as Premier he requested Parliament to "vote him full powers," stating "whoever stands against the government will be punished.... The nation is waiting. We will not give it words but deeds." The powers were voted. Parliament has met periodically since but has confined itself to confirming executive orders and decrees and has now voted its own final dissolution—with cheers.

In order that there can be no doubt as to its antithesis to Liberalism, we may well accept Premier Mussolini's definition of Fascism.[9]

> ...Fascism combats the whole complex of democratic ideology and repudiates it.... Fascism denies that the majority can direct human society, it denies that numbers alone can govern by means of periodical consultation....Fascism denies in democracy the absurd conventional untruth of political equality...and the myth of "happiness" and indefinite progress.... Fascism has taken up an attitude of complete opposition to the doctrines of Liberalism born in the political field and the field of economics...let it be pointed out that all political hopes of the present day are anti-Liberal.

> Granted that the nineteenth century was the century of Socialism, of Liberalism, and of Democracy...it may rather be expected that this will be a century of authority, a century of the left, a century of Fascism; for if the nineteenth century was a century of individualism (Liberalism always signifying individualism) it may be expected that this will be the century of collectivism, and hence the century of the state....

> The Fascist state is an embodied will to power and government; the Roman tradition is here an ideal of force in action...this fact explains many aspects of the practical working of the régime, the character of many forces in the state, and the necessarily severe measures that must be taken against those who would oppose this spontaneous and inevitable movement of Italy in the twentieth century, and would oppose it by recalling the outworn ideology of the nineteenth century—repudiated wheresoever there has been the courage to undertake great experiments of social and political transformations.... If every age has its own characteristic doctrine, there are a thousand signs that point to Fascism as the characteristic doctrine of our time.

The political organization of Italy today is a complete dictatorship supported by one political party to the forcible

---

[9]*Enciclopedia Italiana*, Vol. 14. Translation of the *Political Quarterly*, London.

exclusion of all others. In respect to the Constitution, Premier Mussolini realistically stated that: "We are not dealing with archeology but politics." The entire organism of local self-government has been abolished. The social organization of Fascism is a recognition of class distinctions and class conflicts with compulsory adjustments to secure "class cooperation." Fascism, as distinguished from Socialism, preserves private property and enterprise as implements of bureaucracy.

The present economic organization of Fascism is based on the "Corporate State," the necessity for which is stated to be "Economic Planning." The Italian word *Corporazioni* currently translated as "corporation" is misleading, as its import is not our business corporation; it is more nearly that of the old English "guild." In more modern expression, which again in American terms is not quite precise, the system is based upon the creation separately of Fascist "labor unions" and Fascist "trade associations" in each industry or calling, whose authority through committees and administrators is binding upon all those engaged in that industry or calling, even though the actual membership of the Association be as small as 10 per cent. These associations or code authorities are judicial persons and have rights not only over their members but over all those who are in the categories which they cover.. All officers are selected from Fascists. The plan is "cooperative" to the extent that coercion from the top produces "voluntary" action. The free labor unions and fraternal associations have been suppressed, and the right to strike and to lockout has been replaced by compulsory determination by labor courts.

These associations are directed and regulated by the appointed Minister of Corporations, with an advisory and coordinating body called the National Council of Corporations, comprising some representatives of the associations as well as of the state. The associations have authority to enforce regulations or codes which have been approved by the Premier or Minister as to the quotas of production, the use of capital, expansion of plant, of wages, and conditions of labor, of prices, and of distribution, and they are enforced upon all those engaged in these callings or industries through fines, imprisonment, or deprivation of the right to do business. This applies as well to what the farmer may plant as to what the factory may produce as to the way the product of either can be disposed of.

The associations are required to engage in moral and political propaganda as well as economic direction. To use a Fascist phrase, they are an "instrument of economic perfection" for their members. One of the constantly reiterated primary purposes of this whole economic organism is to bring about "National Planning"—which is frankly interpreted to mean government dictation of economic life. To use again a Fascist phrase, "The National Council disciplines the interests of the categories with a view to national prosperity."[10]

The whole openly represents a regimented economy dictated by government through bureaucracy. The Italian leaders frankly and realistically state that such is the case and that it is incompatible with and unworkable in a liberal state, because its operation necessitates the sacrifice to the state of fundamental rights of personal liberty. As independent legislative action, investigation, free speech, free press, free assembly, free elections—every form of political life except

[10]Giuseppe Bottai, Minister of Fascist Corporations, 1931.

Fascism—have all been forbidden and rigorously suppressed by imprisonment and banishment, it is natural to conclude that Fascist experience has demonstrated what our deductions must be, that such an organization of society can only be held and administered by the extinction of the agencies of criticism and correction, and by the destruction of personal liberties through suppression and terrorization.

It may be observed that despite the fact that the dictatorship with this philosophy of regimentation and of "National Planning" has been in action for over ten years, it has not been able to ward off the same forces of economic disorganization as we have had to meet in the United States. From 1929 to 1933 in Italy wholesale prices, agricultural prices, exports and imports, and real wages have been almost identical in their proportional decline with those of the United States. Likewise, unemployment has been a great and increasing burden upon the people. Having dictatorial powers, the Italian government summarily suppressed the circulation of alarming statements which might cause runs upon banks, and to that extent it avoided some of our difficulties. But large measures of support to the financial system were required. The banks were compelled to support the stock market, and government credit was furnished to them for the purpose. In the acute period of 1931, and again in 1933, the banks, becoming overloaded with securities, had to be relieved by governmental action, and a series of new and supplemental credit agencies had to be created by the government to prevent financial collapse.

In reckoning what are the values and necessities of this system to Italy in preference to Liberalism, we must recognize that the concept of Liberty had never been strongly developed in the Italian people. The extent of poverty, class stratification, illiteracy, sectionalism, the tradition of the Imperial Roman State with its autocratic principle, the comparative recency of its liberal tradition, had prevented much of the penetrative value of Liberalism. The standards of living, the diffusion of wealth, the development of welfare activities for the people as a whole, and restraints upon industrial oppression were far behind those of the United States. Apparently the economic condition of many people of Italy has been improved. It must be borne in mind, however, that they started from a level below and still remain far below American standards.

Moreover, after the war the difficulties of the Italian State were greatly increased by Socialism and Communism and the failure of any party unity. But as to whether the "emergency" was as great as represented, we have only the protagonists' view, and necessarily the rise of most dictatorship in history has justified itself upon saving the country in "emergency." Whether the Italian State would have equally overcome its difficulties had it renounced Socialism and Communism and continued under Liberal forms, or whether, in the high view, it has not lost more through sacrifice of freedom than it has gained from regimented economic life, is not the purpose of this inquiry. What we are interested in is whether Fascism is better for us. And in this we know of it mostly through its proponents, because of the suppression of criticism from within and of free investigation from without.

Even upon this evidence there is not nor ever has been the remotest social, economic, or governmental reason for our adopting it, or entering upon a slide toward it, for that accelerated with every step. Fascism is the flat contradiction of the Declaration of Independence, the Bill of Rights, the Liberal insistence that progress moves in freedom with the help of doubt and criticism. It means the destruction of self-government and of all checks upon incompetent or ruthless tyranny. Americans, unfamiliar with Italy today, do not know how safe a thing Liberty is both for soul and body.

NAZIISM

The rise of Chancellor Hitler and the Nationalist Socialist Party mark, as did Fascism in Italy, the revolt of the middle class. In Germany the impulses sprang from resentment at the terms of the treaties, the miseries of war and inflation, the detestation of financial exploitation which arose particularly out of inflation, and from Socialism and Communism. Despite its name, Herr Hitler's party is violently anti-socialistic. It is not only extremely nationalistic but extends its vision beyond national borders to extreme racialism, from which arises the inhumane persecution of the Jews.

Herr Hitler rose to power by constitutional steps, but within sixty days the Reichstag, upon demand, voted practically unlimited power to the Chancellor and in effect abandoned all legislative responsibility. Most of the processes have followed the Fascist pattern—the unlimited dictatorship, the terrorization, the suppression of all local self-government, the emphasis on class differentiation, the forcible abolition of the craft labor unions, the National Planning, the regimented economic life, the practical adoption of the system of the "Corporate State," the suppression of free speech, free press, and free assembly, the abolition of all guaranties of personal liberty under the constitution of the Republic.

It may be emphasized again that all of these systems of society—Socialism, Communism, Fascism, and Naziism—have some features in common. All these various forms of the collectivist philosophy merely differ in degree and kinds of servitudes. The daily demonstrations in practice in Italy, Germany, Russia, and elsewhere are proof enough that regimentation of men cannot maintain itself against the will of men to be free except by drastic repression and tyranny.

Chapter 6

National Regimentation

The origins, character, and affinities of the Regimentation theory of economics and government, its impacts upon true American Liberalism, and its departures from it can best be determined by an examination of the actions taken and measures adopted in the United States during recent months.

It is not from oratory either in advocacy of this philosophy or equally in denial of it that we must search for its significance. That is to be found by an examination of the actual steps taken and proposed.

From this examination we may dismiss measures of relief of distress from depression, and reform of our laws regulating business when such actions conform to the domain of true Liberty, for these are, as I shall indicate, not Regimentation.

CONCENTRATION OF POWER

The first step of economic Regimentation is a vast centralization of power in the Executive. Without tedious recitation of the acts of the Congress delegating powers over the people to the Executive or his assistants, and omitting relief and regulatory acts, the powers which have been assumed include, directly or indirectly, the following:

To debase the coin and set its value; to inflate the currency; to buy and sell gold and silver; to buy Government bonds, other securities, and foreign exchange; to seize private stocks of gold at a price fixed by the Government; in effect giving to the Executive the power to "manage" the currency;

To levy sales taxes on food, clothing, and upon goods competitive to them (the processing tax) at such times and in such amounts as the Executive may determine;

To expend enormous sums from the appropriations for public works, relief, and agriculture upon projects not announced to the Congress at the time appropriations were made;

To create corporations for a wide variety of business activities, heretofore the exclusive field of private enterprise;

To install services and to manufacture commodities in competition with citizens;

To buy and sell commodities; to fix minimum prices for industries or dealers; to fix handling charges and therefore profits; to eliminate "unfair" trade practices;

To allot the amount of production to individual farms and factories and the character of goods they shall produce; to destroy commodities; to fix stocks of commodities to be on hand;

To estop expansion or development of industries or of specific plant and equipment;

To establish minimum wages; to fix maximum hours and conditions of labor;

To impose collective bargaining;

To organize administrative agencies outside of Civil Service requirements;

To abrogate the effect of the anti-trust acts;

To raise and lower the tariffs and to discriminate between nations in their application;

To abrogate certain governmental contracts without compensation or review by the courts;

To enforce most of these powers where they affect the individual by fine and imprisonment through prosecution in the courts, with a further reserved authority in many trades through license to deprive men of their business and livelihood without any appeal to the courts.

Most of these powers may be delegated by the Executive to any appointee and the appointees are mostly without the usual confirmation by the Senate. The staffs of most of the new organizations are not selected by the merit requirements of the Civil Service. These direct or indirect powers were practically all of them delegated by the Congress to the Executive upon the representation that they were "emergency" authorities, and most of them are limited to a specific time for the purpose of bringing about national recovery from the depression.

At some time or place all of these authorities already have been used. Powers once delegated are bound to be used, for one step drives to another. Moreover, some group somewhere gains benefits or privilege by the use of every power. Once a power is granted, therefore, groups begin to exert the pressure necessary to force its use. Once used, a vested interest is created which thereafter opposes any relaxation and thereby makes for permanence. But beyond this, many steps once taken set economic forces in motion which cannot be retrieved. Already we have witnessed all these processes in action.

The manner of use of these powers and their immediate impacts upon the concepts of true American Liberty may first be examined under the five groups or ideas into which they naturally fall—Regimented Industry and Commerce, Regimented Agriculture, Government in Competitive Business, Managed Currency and Credit, and Managed Foreign Trade.

REGIMENTED INDUSTRY AND COMMERCE

The application of Regimentation to business has made great strides. We now have the important branches of industry and commerce organized into trade groups, each presided over by a committee of part trade and part government representatives heading up through an "Administrator" to the Executive. There are a number of advisory boards for various purposes whose personnel is part trade and part bureaucratic. More than 400 separate trades have been organized, estimated to cover 1,500,000 establishments or about 90 per cent of the business of the country outside of farming.

In this organization of commerce and industry the trades were called upon to propose codes of management for their special callings. Parts of each of these codes are, however, imposed by law, whether the trades propose them or not. The determination as to who represents the trade is reserved to the Executive, and in the absence of a satisfactory proposal he may himself make and promulgate a code. He may force deletion of any proposed provision and may similarly impose provisions and exceptions.

Each of the codes is directly or indirectly binding upon every member of the trade whether he was represented in its making or whether he agreed or not. It has force of statutory law, enforceable by fine and jail through the courts. Originally the Executive could require every member of a trade to tale out a license to do business. In this license he could impose the conditions under which persons may continue to do business. The Executive could revoke a license without affording any appeal to or protection of the courts. This licensing power has expired in general industry but still stands as an authority to the Secretary of Agriculture over all producers, processors and dealers in agricultural products. This is a very considerable part of American business. Except as an example of the extent of violation of freedom this licensing provision is not important, as the other provisions and methods are sufficiently coercive without it.

The codes impose minimum wages and maximum hours and provide, further, for collective agreement with labor as to wages and conditions of work beyond the minimums. By far the major use of the codes is, however, devoted to the elimination of "unfair competitive practices." This expression or its counterpart, "fair competition," has been interpreted not alone to cover "unethical" practices, but to include the forced elimination of much normal functioning of competition through reduced production, the prevention of plant expansion, and a score of devices for fixing of minimum prices and trade margins. From so innocent terms as "fair competition" and its counterpart have been builded this gigantic dictation—itself a profound example of the growth of power when once granted.

In this mobilization there has been constant use of the term "cooperation." However, the law itself makes important parts of the codes compulsory and by their indirect powers can impose any of them. As practical persons observing their workings, we may dismiss voluntary impulses as the motivation of this organization. At best it is "coercive cooperation." Free will and consent, the essential elements in cooperation, have not often been present. The spirit of the whole process has been coercive, principally through the overshadowing authority to impose the codes and the terror of effective deprival of any man of his business and his livelihood. The mere fact of charges made by bureaucrats can act to deprive him of his reputation. Where such authority arises among free men is difficult to discern.

Ample evidence of coercion is found in the bludgeoning of many important code conferences, in the changes forced in some codes, from which there was no appeal or refuge; in the incitement of public boycott; and in the contracts required in all dealings with the government itself. One need but read the vast flood of propaganda, of threat and pressure, the daily statements of the administering officials, and follow the actions of "compliance" boards and other agencies, in every town or village, to confirm the fact of coercion. Men have been fined or ordered to jail for the crime of selling goods or services at lower prices than their competitors. One of the sad results in the arraying of neighbor against neighbor, group against group, all grasping for desperate advantage from the law.

There are "unfair practices" which need reform because of the failure of some States to rise fully to their responsibilities. The codes have served admirably to reduce child labor by about 25 per cent, and they have eliminated sweating in certain trades. They have eliminated some unethical business practices, but they have stimulated many more new ones through "chiseling." This sort of reform is within the powers of the States, and laws to this purpose have been enacted by most of them. If we have determined that we must nationally force these measures on delinquent States and if they be within the constitutional powers of the Federal Government, then they can be carried out by specific law enforced by the judicial arm and do not require the regimentation of the economic system. But in practical working only a small part of the codes are devoted to these ends.

The most effective part of code operations are devoted to limitation of real competition. It is true that the law provided that there should be no monopolies or monopolistic practices. The major aspiration of those seeking to avoid the anti-trust acts always has been precisely the fixing of minimum prices and restriction of output, and these objectives, so earnestly yearned for in some quarters, now have been imposed by law. The economic results, so far as the trades and consumers are concerned, are about the same as if the anti-trust acts had been abolished. Naturally, if these industrial regiments hold to discipline they are at once constituted as complete guild monopolies as any in the Elizabethan period, from which we derived much of our American antagonism to monopoly.

But an equally regrettable social effect has been that the imposition of larger costs, and the fixing of minimum prices and trade differentials crashed down at once on smaller units of business. If persisted in there can be no disunity of these processes in the long run but a gradual absorption of business by the larger units. All this is in fact the greatest legal mechanism ever devised for squeezing the smaller competitor out of action, easily and by the majesty of the law. Yet the small business is the very fibre of our community life.

Over it all is now the daily dictation by Government in every town and village every day in the week, of how men are to conduct their daily lives—under constant threat of jail, for crimes which have no moral turpitude. All this is the most stupendous invasion of the whole spirit of Liberty that the nation has witnessed since the days of Colonial America.

REGIMENTED AGRICULTURE

The farmer is the most tragic figure in our present situation. From the collapse of war inflation, from boom, from displacement of work-animals by mechanization, from the breakdown of foreign markets, from the financial debacle of Europe, and from the drought, he has suffered almost beyond human endurance.

Instead of temporarily reducing the production of marginal lands by measures of relief pending world recovery, the great majority of farmers were regimented to reduce production from the fertile lands. The idea of a subsidy to a farmer to reduce his production in a particular "staple commodity" was expanded by requiring a contract that he would follow order from the Secretary of Agriculture in the production of other "staple commodities." Voluntary action was further submerged by threats that if he did not sign up he would have difficulty in obtaining credit.

The whole process has been a profound example both of how bureaucracy, once given powers to invade Liberty, proceeds to fatten and enlarge its activities, and of how departures from practical human nature and economic experience soon find themselves so entangled as to force more and more violent steps.

To escape the embarrassment of the failure to reduce production by these methods, still further steps were taken into coercion and regimentation. Yet more "staples," not authorized by the Congress to be controlled when the contracts were signed, were added to the list. A further step was to use the taxing power on excess production of cotton and to set quotas on sugar. Directly or indirectly, on many farms these devices create a privilege and destroy a right. Since only those who have had the habit of producing cotton and some other commodities may now do so, they are given a monopoly and any other farmer is precluded from turning his land to that purpose.

And recently still further powers were demanded from the Congress by which the last details of complete coercion and dictation might be exerted not alone to farmers but to everyone who manufactures and distributes farm products. That all this is marching to full regimentation of thirty millions of our agricultural population is obvious enough.

But we are told that the farmer must, in the future, sacrifice Liberty to economic comfort. The economic comfort up to date may be questioned, as likewise the longevity of any comfort, for the basic premise is not tenable.[11]

The stark fact is that if part of Liberty to a particular farmer is removed, the program must move quickly into complete dictation, for there are here no intermediate stages. The nature of agriculture makes it impossible to have regimentation up to a point and freedom of action beyond that point. Either the farmer must use his own judgment, must be free to plant and sell as he wills, or he must take orders from the corporal put above him.

The whole thesis behind this program is the very theory that man is but the pawn of the state. It is a usurpation of the primary liberties of men by government.

GOVERNMENT IN COMPETITIVE BUSINESS

The deliberate entry of the government into business in competition with the citizen, or in replacement of private

[11]Thomas Jefferson once said, "Were we directed from Washington when to sow, and when to reap, we should soon want bread." *Autobiography*. Vol 1, p. 113.

enterprise, (other than as a minor incident to some major public purpose), is regimentation of the people directly into a bureaucracy. That, of course, is Socialism in the connotation of any sociologist or economist and is confirmed as such today by the acclaim of the Socialists.

As an instance we may cite the Tennessee Valley Authority, where the major purpose of the government is the purchase, construction, operation, transmission, and sale of electricity in the Tennessee Valley and neighborhood, together with the manufacture and merchandising of appliances, fertilizers, chemicals, and other commodities. Other instances occur where Public Works money has been allotted to the erection of dams and reservoirs, and to the construction of power plants, the major purpose of which is to undertake the production and sale of electricity in competition with the citizen.

There have long been instances of public works for the real major purpose of flood control, irrigation, or navigation, which produce water-power as a by-product. Here, if the government leases this power under proper protections to the public, the competition with the citizen is avoided. Here is one of the definite boundaries between Liberty and Socialism. Under Liberty, the citizen must have strong regulation of the rates and profits of power companies to protect him from oppression by the operator of a natural monopoly. But where the government deliberately enters into the power business as a major purpose in competition with the citizen—that is Socialism.

Still other instances of government competition with citizens are five corporations created by the government under the laws of Delaware, which are engaged in various competitive businesses covering the manufacture and merchandising of commodities.

These entries into Socialism were not an important emergency call to relieve unemployment. The total expenditures provided will employ but a very small percentage of the unemployed. In fact, the threat to private enterprise will probably stifle employment of more men in the damage to existing enterprises. There is already ample private capacity to supply any of the commodities they produce, whether electricity, fertilizers, rum, or furniture. Whatever their output is, its production will displace that much private employment somewhere. We have only to examine a fragment of the statements of their sponsors to find that their purposes, although sometimes offered as employment, are in fact further blows pounding in the wedge of Socialism as a part of regimenting the people into a bureaucracy.

There are measures in banking and credit which might be discussed under this heading but they are dealt with elsewhere. And in another chapter of this book I have dealt at length with the effect and destiny of Socialism.

MANAGED CURRENCY AND CREDIT

The scope of this survey does not include a full examination of monetary, fiscal, and credit policies. I am here concerned solely with profound departures from Liberty.

Without entering upon the recent technical monetary steps taken, it may be said at once that the intent of the powers given to alter the unit value of currency is, by "managed currency," to enable the government to change from time to time the purchasing power of the currency for all commodities, wages, salaries, and income. One underlying intent of the monetary measures was the transfer of income and property from one individual to another, or from one group to another, upon an enormous scale without judicial processes. Whether the theory under this assumption will produce the effects intended or not, the intent is definitely expressed.

REPUDIATION OF DEBT

The installation of managed currency required the repudiation of the government contract to meet its obligations in gold.[12]   And the repudiation of the gold clause extended

[12]"Why are we going off the gold standard? With nearly 40 per cent of the entire gold supplies of the world, why are we going off the gold standard? With all the ear-marked gold, with all the securities of ours that they hold, foreign governments could withdraw in total less than $700,000,000 of our gold, which would leave us an ample fund of gold, in the extremist case, to maintain gold payments both abroad and at home.

"To me, the suggestion that we may devalue the fold dollar 50 per cent means national repudiation. To me it means dishonor; in my conception of it, it is immoral.

"All the legalistic arguments which the lawyers of the Senate, men of eminent ability and refinement, may make here, or have made here, have not dislodged from my mind the irrevocable conviction that it is immoral, and that it means not only a contravention of my party's platform in that respect, but of the promises of party spokesmen during the campaign.

"Mr. President, there was never any necessity for a gold embargo. There is no necessity for making statutory criminals of citizens of the United States who may please to take property in the shape of gold or currency out of banks and use it for their own purposes as they may please.

.   .   .   .

"If there were need to go off the gold standard, very well, I would say let us go off the gold standard; but there has been no need for that."

—*From the Senate remarks of Mr. Glass, Senator from Virginia, April 27, 1933.*

much farther than repudiation of government obligations alone, for it changed the value of all contracts between citizens far beyond the present appreciation of the citizen of its possible results—if it shall prove to have the effect which was intended.

Onc of the major objectives stated was to reduce unbearable debt. It was asserted that the value of the dollar as represented in its purchasing power for goods or services had changed from its value when the original bargains of debt were made. Under this operation the citizens were regimented into two groups, debtors and creditors. An empirical and universal amount of 40 to 50 per cent was set as the degree of shift in the value of all property to the debtor regiment from the creditor regiment.

This act involved the widest responsibility which the government bears to its citizens, and that individuals bear toward each other. For fidelity to contract, unless determined unconscionable by an independent tribunal, is the very integrity of Liberty and of any economic society. Where the debt of certain groups such as part of the farmers and home-owners becomes oppressive, and its social results to the entire nation are of vital importance, such a service is justified, but it should not have been undertaken at the particular cost of those honest creditors whose savings have been thus invested but should have been a special burden upon the whole nation. But the injustice is far wider than this.

These monetary acts extend the assumption of unbearable debt over the whole of the private and public debts of the nation. That this attempt at universal shift of 40 to 50 per cent of the value of all debts was neither necessary nor just can be demonstrated in a few sentences. The theory mistakenly assumed that the distorted prices and values at the depth of a banking panic were permanent. It assumed that the recovery from depression in progress through the world would not extend to the United States. Of even more importance, this theory also assumed that every single debt had become oppressive; that every single creditor had benefited by about one-half since the initial bargain; that every single debtor had lost by this amount; that no debtor could carry out his initial bargain; and that the respective rights of every debtor and every creditor in every kind of property should be shifted from debtor to creditor without any inquiry or process of justice. Debt is an individual thing, not a mass transaction. The circumstances of every debt vary.

Certainly the Government cannot contend that its debt was oppressive. No man has yet stated that the Government could not have paid its obligations in full. It was not insolvent. It was not bankrupt.

In large areas of private debt the borrower was amply able to meet his obligations. In other great areas he had already profited by large dividends or earnings, or otherwise by the use of the savings of lenders which he had deliberately solicited. A huge part of the bond issues of railways, of power companies, of industrial companies, of foreign governments, current commercial debt, the bank deposits, urban mortgages and what not belong to these categories.

The evidence of the volume of debts which require governmental relief as a social necessity does not by any conceivable calculation indicate more than a very minor percentage of the total public and private debt. Extensive provisions for the adjustment between individuals of their debts were made by new facilities under the bankruptcy acts and the further relief measures provided through the use of government credit.

But let us examine the injustice under this managed currency more particularly. In a great category where debt required adjustment there had already been many compromises between debtors and investors, as witness the many reorganizations of urban building loans, and corporate and other obligations, which were the products of inflation. The people's savings invested in these cases are required, by depreciation of the dollar, to submit to a still further loss.

Most lending is ultimately from savings which mean somebody's self-denial of the joy of spending today in order to provide for the future. But the borrower is often enough a person who secured these joys and is now to be relieved of part payment, although a large part of these borrowers are able to pay. The man who borrowed from an insurance company to build himself a more expensive and enjoyable house has secured these joys at the cost of the policyholder, who had hoped by self-denial to escape dependency. This applies equally to the huge debt of industrial and commercial businesses which profited by their borrowings from the policyholder and the depositor in a savings bank.

Those self-denying investors—the thrifty of the nation—who were willing to accept a low rate of interest in order to obtain the maximum security, and under this theory to have the purchasing value of their savings now shrunken in exactly the same ratio as the avaricious who received extortionate rates, or the reckless who took high risks. The holders of hard-won savings—the widow's mite—invested in 3 1/4 per cent first mortgage industrial bonds are called upon to sacrifice the same proportion as the holders of 7 per cent third mortgages. By the transfer of values from the first mortgage bondholder to the common stockholder the security of these speculative bonds is even increased. At once we see the evidence of this in the marked advance in the prices of these speculative debts. This disregard of prudence and this benefit to recklessness particularly penalizes a very large part of insurance and the great public endowment assets.

Ten billions of endowments in educational, hospitalization, and welfare activities—creditors whose debtors are mostly corporations and governments—are to be depleted in purchasing power. These endowed institutions give the leadership necessary to all our vast complex of public institutions. Yet if this theory eventuate, their activities must diminish by 40 per cent.

Furthermore, if this theory shall succeed, in the great bulk of industrial debt, the empirical reduction of purchasing power of the regiments of bondholders transfers this purchasing power to the regiments of common stockholders. Any inspection of who are the rank and file in these regiments will at once demonstrate the double injustice. The holders of bonds are largely the insurance company, the savings bank depositor, the small investor, and the endowed institution.

If this intent of devaluation shall eventuate, the transfer of property by government fiat from sixty million insurance policyholders to ten million stockholders is not even diffusion of wealth. It is further concentration of wealth. As a matter of fact, any survey of the total results would show (if the theory of these acts works out) that it will benefit the richest members of the community, because their property is, in the main, in equities. The hardship will fall upon the great mass of the people who are indirect holders of obligations through their savings in insurance, in savings bank deposits, as well as those who directly hold bonds and mortgages. That is, in our modern American economy the rich are more largely the holders of equities and those of moderate means more largely the holders of obligations. Thus the rich hereby become richer, the poor poorer. Monetary shifts in their very nature are mostly irretrievable. There can be little turning back.

THE CONSEQUENCES OF MANAGED CURRENCY

In "managed currency"—a power of government fiat over the values of wages, income, and property—we find many by-products from the invasion of Liberty. To some academic theorists the Commodity Dollar may be perfect. But for thousands of years the whole human race has esteemed gold as the final gauge of values. Whether the sign of the index number, which is the kernel of this branch of "planned economics," be theoretically a better gauge or not, the fact remains that gold is a matter of faith. Men will long delay full faith in an abstraction such as the commodity index, with its uncertainties of political manipulation or of Executive determination. This has a pertinent application today. Those people who are employed are heaping up their savings. Yet these potential investors have hitherto hesitated to loan their savings over a long period, not knowing with what they may be paid in years to come nor what their rights may be. The durable goods industries are dependent upon this investment in the form of long-term credits. At the same time the country has an accumulated need for a vast amount of homes and equipment. As these credits are much restricted, vast numbers out of work suffer the injustice of cruel delays in otherwise possible employment.

GOVERNMENT DICTATION OF CREDIT

How far Regimentation of banking and the government dictation of credit through various government agencies may extend is not yet clear. There are national stresses in which the government must support private financial institutions, but it is unnecessary for it to enter into competitive business to accomplish this. And lest the government step over the line into Socialism this support must be limited to activities where there is no competition, or so organized as ultimately to be absorbed into the hands of private ownership. The Original Reconstruction Finance Corporation is an example of the former and the Federal Reserve Banks, the Home Loan Banks, the Federal Land Banks, of the latter. There are, however, some of the new financial agencies and some used being made of the old agencies which forecast occupation beyond these fields, and threaten dictation as to who may and who may not have credit. The threat to farmers of withholding credit to force them to sign crop contracts with the government is a current example of possibilities.

The reduction of the independence of the Federal Reserve Board and the Farm Loan System to dependency upon the political administration, the provisions for appointment of officials in the banks by government agencies, and certain provisions in the new regulatory acts, all at least give enormous power of "managed credit."

If the purpose of all these activities is to enable the government to dictate which business or individual shall have credit and which shall not, we will witness a tyranny never before contemplated in our history.

The wounds to Liberty—and to justice upon which Liberty rests—in these monetary actions and policies are thus myriad. It is again a specific demonstration of a social philosophy defensible only on the ground that the citizen is but a pawn of the state—the negation of the whole philosophy of Liberty. Executive power over the coin is one of the oldest components of despotism.

MANAGED FOREIGN TRADE

There is another segment of National Regimentation into which these other segments immediately force us, and that is foreign trade. The whole theory of controlled domestic production and prices falls to the ground unless imports also are rigidly controlled. As managed industry and agriculture operate the nation must be surrounded with barriers which insulate it from economic currents beyond its borders. Going off the gold standard theoretically raised most tariffs 40 per cent, and theoretically imposed that barrier against goods on the free list as well. The additions to tariffs by the amount of the processing taxes are further indications of the inexorable mounting of trade barriers under such a plan.

There can be no escape from constant international difficulties. These difficulties were great enough when the government made a fixed tariff upon 34 per cent of the imports based upon a simple proposal of differences in cost of production at home and abroad, and allowed 66 per cent of its imports to enter freely, and when it treated every nation alike. But when, in effect, it places barriers of one sort or another on the whole 100 per cent of imports by currency and exchange manipulation, when these barriers are to shift with every government-made price in industry, when they are to be made to vary by favor in trading with different nations, through reciprocal tariffs, then there is no doubt we also have joined in the world economic war already disastrously in progress. That economic war is steadily drying up the outlets for human initiative. The hop of the world in an economy of plenty through the huge increase in productive power which science has given us threatens to be stifled by these processes of nationalism and regimentation.

Men can haggle with each other in the markets of the world and there is no ripple in international good-will, but when governments do the haggling, then the spirit of antagonism between peoples is thrice inflamed.

This brief survey of examples of experience up to this time is sufficient to make clear the definition and nature of National Regimentation and its progress in the United States. There are other channels in which our economic and social life is being regimented which could be developed. These instances are certainly sufficient to show that its very spirit is government direction, management, and dictation of social and economic life. It is a vast shift from the American concept of human rights which even the government may not infringe to those social philosophies where men are wholly subjective to the state. It is a vast casualty to Liberty if it shall be continued.

Chapter 7

The Consequences to Liberty of Continued Regimentation

The most gigantic step morally, spiritually, economically, and governmentally that a nation can take is to shift its fundamental philosophic and social ideas. The entry upon such a movement presents the most fateful moment in the history of a people.

But before entering upon the subject of the further and broader consequences of National Regimentation or the adoption of other social philosophies in American life, I shall clear the road of some unrelated subjects.

EMERGENCY ACTIONS EXCLUDED

I am not here discussing any of the current measures except so far as our present experience of them illustrates the effect which they have upon Liberty. Although I hold that emergency neither necessitates nor justifies departures from fundamental liberties—and incidentally will in the end retard recovery itself through disturbance of confidence in the future—I am not here dealing with temporary actions as such. Overshadowing temporary actions, whether wise or unwise, is the far larger issue. An emergency program for recovery is one thing, but to implant a new social philosophy in

American life in conflict with the primary concepts of American Liberty is quite another thing.

We are told today by men high in our government both legislative and administrative that the social organization which we have developed over our whole history is "outworn" and "must be abandoned." We have been told that it has "failed." We are told of "outworn traditions," that we have come to the "end of an era," that we are passing through a "bloodless revolution." We are also told that the American System "is in ruins," that we must "build on the ruins of the past a new structure." It is advocated now that many of the emergency measures shall be "consolidated" and made "permanent." We should therefore earnestly and dispassionately examine what the pattern of this transformation of the economic, social, and governmental system is to be, and what the ultimate effect of its continuance would be upon our national life.

RELIEF OF DISTRESS

Among the important measures of government, both in the present Administration and in the last, are a large number devoted to relief of distress, both personal and institutional; the expansion of public works; revisions of the older laws regulating business; the reinforcement of State regulation by Federal acts; and the support of cooperative action among the citizens by temporary use of Federal credit. Many of the additional measures undertaken in these directions during the past months are admirable if properly administrated.

Proper action in relief of distress in inherent in the social vision of the true American System. No American should go hungry or cold if he is willing to work. Under our system relief is first the obligation of the individual to his neighbors then of institutions, then of local communities, and then of the State governments. The moment that need exceeds the honest capacities of the local agencies, then they must have the support of the Federal Government as the final reservoir of national strength.

This includes an indirect relief through public works, direct relief when all other measures have failed, and proper support to financial institutions when failures will reduce large numbers to destitution. We may not approve the current methods of applying relief. We may feel that some of these methods undermine State and local responsibility; that they are wasteful or futile or alive with corruption. We may learn that they may be misused, by subversion or the electorate through partisan organization, to create future artillery against the walls of Liberty. But even so, these are correctable abuses and lesser questions, evanescent in the long view of national life.

REGULATION OF ABUSES

The depression has brought to the surface a number of weaknesses and abuses in the economic system. I deal elsewhere more fully with the whole subject of abuse of Liberty. For this immediate discussion I may state that reform and revision of our older regulatory laws in banking, commodity and stock markets, transportation, utilities and natural resource industries are absolutely necessary. So long as these revisions conform to the conditions of Liberty there can be no difference of opinion except as to method. All reform entails some degree of experiment. I have no fear of experiments which take account of experience, do not remake the errors of history, and do not set out to experiment with the principles of Liberty. We may feel that some reform measures do not reach to the heart of the problems they undertake to solve; that they are in part punitive rather than constructive; that they are in part impractical of producing the desired result; that in attempting to suppress a dozen scoundrels they are retarding the normal and active flow of economic life among a thousand honest men, and are thus retarding recovery from the depression. But we must remember that reform is a hard horse to ride in the blinding storm of world war liquidation.

"NATIONAL PLANNING"

There have run through all the dissertations of the past months the slogans and promise of "National Planning," "Planned Economy," or "Permanent Planning."[13] Obviously these phrases have been given a new meaning. They do not mean mere charts and blueprints. They mean execution as well. They do not mean only the planning and executing of the normal unctions of government. Obviously there is included also regimentation of industry and agriculture, management of currency and credit, government competition with business, management of foreign trade, and many other activities, all to be definitely dictated by officials acting from Washington. That is the coercive execution of plans for the daily economic and social lives of the people.

---

[13]It has been said that statesmanship often consists of presenting old forms under new names. But modern social agitation seems to have reversed this procedure to presenting new forms of their own coinage under familiar terms. This use of the term "national planning" is not alone in this advent. To it may be added the new meanings given such terms as "Capitalism," "Liberalism," "Democratic Processes," "Sound Money," "*Laissez Faire*," "Rugged Individualism," "Regulation," "Control," "Readjustment," "Cooperation," and "Emergency."

We have been engaged in planning, and the execution of plans, within the proper functions of government ever since the first days of George Washington's administration. We have planned and executed public school systems, safeguards to public health, conservation of national resources, the reclamation of desert lands, vast river and harbor development, a magnificent system of highways and public buildings, the creation of parks, the beautification of cities, and a thousand other activities in every state, town, and village. We have planned and executed laws controlling semi-monopolies and maintenance of competition. We have set up the Federal Reserve System, the Land Banks, the Home Loan Banks. We planned and built the Panama Canal. The government has cooperated with the people in planning and executing a great system of railways, of airways, of merchant marine. It has gone further. The government through its constituted officials has cooperated in furthering great social activities, by determining facts and by assisting organizations to make plans for social advancement, to create standards, to coordinate thought and stimulate effort.

Nor have our non-governmental activities been without plan and execution by the people themselves, as witness the gigantic physical equipment of the nation and its intellectual progress. If this vast achievement was not the result of conscious planning, then it is eloquent proof that these things come spontaneously out of our American System.

No civilization has hitherto ever seen such a growth of voluntary associative activities in every form of planning, co-ordination and cooperation of effort, the expression of free men. It comes naturally, since the whole system builded on Liberty is a stimulant to plan and progress. The unparalleled rise of the American man and woman was not alone the result of riches in lands, forests, or mines; it sprang from ideals and philosophic ideas out of which plans, and the execution of them, are stimulated by the forces of freedom.

The assertion is made that these Regimentations or National Planning are merely extended cooperation. Civilization dawned when the first group of men acted in cooperation, and men have ever since divided over how far they should be forced to group action or whether they should join of their own free will. Our American civilization is based upon the maximum of free will in an ordered Liberty. Aside from the very philosophy of Liberty, the practicalities are that when free men come together in economic life they pool a wealth of practical experience and conscientious responsibility. They are compelled to find workable methods of cooperation. Over every deliberation hangs the sobering threat of personal loss for a wrong decision. There is no one to whom the cost of error may be passed. But under coercive cooperation by government, the final determination of method for the joint action is made not by men of large experience in practical affairs, but by government agents—often by men wholly lacking in both vision and ability. The bureaucrat is above accountability so long as his political support holds. Cooperation appraises its methods and consequences step by step and pays its bills as it goes. Bureaucracy rushes headlong into visions of the millennium and sends the bill to the Treasury.

The methods of planning progress cannot be through governmental determination of when and how much a factory may be operated, what the farmer may plant or sell, or any other of the processes of regimentation. The forces of true cooperation may be less immediate in their results than coercion, but they are more permanent, for they do not wither the real impulses of progress and they do not atrophy the responsibility of the citizen.

There are transcendent obstacles to the successful working of these ideas of coercive National Planning or National Regimentation of our economic and social life. The first is the inability to command the omniscient genius required to plan and coordinate and direct the operation of the economic and social machine. This is true even if the government enjoyed the powers of complete dictatorship as in the cases of Fascism and Communism. The second and higher obstacle is created when these ideas are mixed with democracy, for they are based upon wholly different conceptions of human rights which instantly clash.

CONFLICT WITH DEMOCRATIC PROCESSES

There arise from this mixture conflicts and interferences which will undermine Liberty by rendering its economic system only partly operative, and they do not give any other system a fair trial. The mixture automatically destroys confidence in the future, which is the essential of our system, and that at once delays initiative and new enterprise. It produces astonishing effects, from the behavior of men part free, which thwart the hoped-for results. It develops surprising conflicts between the regiments created, because of the inability of any human mind to coordinate such vast plans and activities. Complete dictatorship is of course abolition of representative government, but even partial regimentation raises at once conflicts which are destructive to it. One result is to drive unceasingly for more drastic steps. Our American System cannot be made to work part free and part regimented. It is a new form of an old conflict. No system can be part dictatorship and part democracy.

We may confirm these observations if we examine actual results of the operations now in progress and if we examine their tendencies toward the future.

THE GROWTH OF BUREAUCRACY

As I have said, the first necessity of this program of National Planning or National Regimentation, whatever may be the name we apply to it, is obviously a vast concentration of political and economic authority in the Executive. All these plans and regiments must be invented. Their execution must be commanded, administered, and enforced by a delegated somebody. Thus overhanging all these organisms of "managed currency," "regimented industry," "government operation," and "regimented agriculture" is the most vital of questions: Who is to invent? Who is to manage? Who is to command these regiments? And above all, who is to coordinate their activities?

It is not enough to answer, "the Government," "the State," or "the Executive." This direction ultimately must be reposed in government bureaus and they are comprised of human beings with dictatorial powers over us all.

These proposals necessitate that a large part of leadership and managerial responsibility and authority in business and agriculture is to be wrenched from the hands of those who have risen to leadership by success and skill in each specialized calling, and placed in the hands of those who appear to merit political power. An enormous extension of bureaucracy is inevitable. Already a host of new government bureaus and nearly two thousand commissions have been established with authority over every trade, and in nearly every town and village. We have witnessed this host of government agents spread out over the land, limiting men's honest activities, conferring largess and benefits, directing, interfering, disseminating propaganda, spying on, threatening the people and prosecuting for a new host of crimes. It is pertinent therefore to inquire shortly into the course and characteristics of bureaucracy, for in the end that is the agency that will rule over us.

CHARACTERISTICS, SELECTION AND HANDICAPS OF BUREAUCRACY

No one with a day's experience in government fails to realize that in all bureaucracies there are three implacable spirits—self-perpetuation, expansion, and an incessant demand for more power. These are human urges and are supported by a conviction, sometimes justified, that they know what is good for us. Nevertheless, these spirits are potent and possess a dictatorial complex. They lead first to subversive influence in elections. They drive always to extension of powers by interpretation of authority, and by more and more legislation. Power is the father of impatience with human faults, and impatience breeds arrogance. In their mass action, they become the veritable exponents of political tyranny.

Above it all there arises the question of how these masters of our farms, our factories, our stores, our daily lives—with power to deprive citizens of property and income or even to send them to jail for selling goods cheaper than a competitor—are to be selected. No one is so foolish as to believe they can be elected. No one believes that genuine judgment and experience to direct economic activities can be determined by written examinations. No one believes that selection by political tests will produce these qualities, but they will be selected for politics nevertheless. Leadership to command in economic life cannot be picked by bureaucracy; it must be ground out in the hard mills of competition. Genius cannot be created by bureaucracy; it must push upward among free men.

And all these proposals of regimentation lay upon bureaucracy a job it cannot competently do in a democracy even did it possess all other qualities. Bureaucracy engaged in the ordinary functions of government, under defined rules, by the building up of precedent and routine and repetitive experience, can become competent. But the moment bureaucracy must show that creative sense, that instant judgment and responsibility with business requires, it becomes hopeless. Does anyone believe that the automobile would have been invented, constantly perfected, and the enormous industry built by a bureaucracy? Or the railroads, or the mines?

Moreover, in a democracy every member of the Congress, every newspaper, is a potential critic, and the accumulative effect upon government agents is to deter willingness to take that responsibility, risk, and adventure which economic activities require every moment of the day. Private industry measures failure in the new sum of accomplishment. Public criticism measures it by one failure only. The inevitable result is to deaden even any initiative, enterprise, efficiency of bureaucracy that might exist.

It is worth remembering, also, that so long as we continue as a democracy, then leading government employees shift every few years to new and inexperienced men— whereas industry thrives only with continuity of leadership.

The ultimate attitude of bureaucracy in Regimentation to democratic principles is indicated by a statement by Signor

Turati, then Secretary General of the Fascist Party, at Bologna in 1929:

> We are tired of being branded as undemocratic, for we certainly are undemocratic if democracy means the conferring of powers on those above by those below. An Army takes its orders, goes out and executed them, dies if necessary, but it does not question these orders, nor does it elect its officers.

Even if we might assume a competent and continuous administration by bureaucrats, we have yet to face the fact that no centralized, coordinating authority interfering with these billions of daily activities and shifting the direction of the deep currents which affect the welfare of everybody, even if it were composed of supermen, ever could hope to remain abreast of the infinite diversity of life and circumstance in this nation of 125,000,000 people. This is being daily proved in the experience of every citizen.

ECONOMIC CONFLICTS

We can test the ability to dictate the economic life of the people, and above all to coordinate these regiments, by observing some of the contradictory, conflicting, and confusing results which we have experienced already in the past months. At the same time we can indicate the surprising effects of human behavior in the mixture of Regimentation with freedom.

Inescapably there is conflict between the idea of the commanders of one regiment that artificial price-rises will increase business activity and employment, and thereby consumption of goods; and the idea of another regimental command that, in order to increase consumption and employment, prices must be kept down.

There are conflicts between artificial price-increases undertaken to restore agriculture to parity with other industry, and those taken to increase prices of the things the farmer buys. Separated from the drought, the result has added practically nothing to agriculture. There is contradiction in destroying food when people are in want. There is direct conflict between the policy of eliminating marginal agriculture on the one hand, and on the other hand, the policy of maintaining marginal production by subsidies and by the expansion of production through reclamation.

Through regimentation of employers, employees, and consumers there are conflicts as to who is to bear the cost of these artificial price rises. The consequent struggles between employers and employees have resulted in more days' labor lost in nine months through strikes than in the whole of the previous three years. The consumer regiments set their buying resistance against the producers, so that consumption slackens and surpluses increase. This is especially evident in perishable agricultural products where the processing tax, by decreasing consumption, has in effect forced back at least part of the tax to the farmer instead of adding it to the consumer.

There is the conflict between lenders and borrowers as to who shall take the risk of unstable currencies, the result of which is to continue unemployment in the durable goods industries. There is a conflict between government absorption of capital by taxes and borrowings from the common pool for the purpose of giving employment, and its urging of private industry to secure from the depleted pool the capital with which it might give employment. There is conflict of plans, on one hand, that the people should spend a larger part of the current income, and steps on the other hand, which frighten them to restrict spendings.

There is a conflict between maintaining antitrust laws and the setting of monopoly under the codes, one result of which is to squeeze out the smaller business and another result is to increase prices and the cost of living and thus to promote strikes to equate wages. There is at least incompatibility between a system which makes its progress through invention and improvement, and governmental action which creates drags upon the competition which alone inspires them. There is inherent conflict between the theory of government limitation of private production, and the government going into business where there is already ample production. There is a conflict between attempts to move industry to the rural districts and the tendency of production to move to urban areas because of fixed regional wages.

Industry is further confused by the government's payment of higher wages for relief than that fixed in the codes. There is inconsistency between commanding increased wages, shorter hours and greater employment in industry, and cuts and dismissals in government service. There is contradiction between repudiation of government obligations under contracts and the insistence by the law that private contracts by observed. There is inconsistency between the stern reprimand for incapacity and dishonesty in administration of industry and the inevitable outbreak of waste, corruption, and spoils where government goes into business.

There is conflict between the theory of one regiment holding to lower tariffs, and to the lending of government money to promote trade, and the theory of another regiment which increases the tariffs and puts on import quotas and currency wars that restrict trade. There is inconsistency between the government denunciation of private lenders of money to foreign countries, and the government itself lending them money.

These are but part of the catalogue, but sufficient for examples.

These are not surprising results, for they represent in part the inability of men to know the destiny of economic forces, artificially created, even if it is all planned in advance; they represent in part the inability of any government to coordinate these artificial forces when set in motion. They represent also another phase of equal importance, and that is the effect of partial regimentation of the economic system. So long as it is partial, human behavior still controls some elements in the individual's interest, and he uses them. And because of all these difficulties there arises an insistent demand for more power, and the danger of further and further assumption of it.

Such is the march of regimentation. The effect upon our liberties needs no amplification.

EFFECT OF GOVERNMENT SPENDING

The seeking of opportunities for expending huge sums of public money, upon the theory that this will prime the economic pump, ignores the fact that the priming water is an exhaustion of the living water of the public credit. And even beyond that, it enfeebles the power delivered to the pump through stifling confidence and enterprise. Its cost in huge budget deficits must ultimately necessitate huge increase in taxes or the manipulation of either currency or credit or all three. Government postponement of paying for these unprecedented expenditures by expending bank credits and then borrowing the expansion has implications which no one can foresee. But so far no nation or individual has been able to squander itself into prosperity. So far as history shows, every such borrowing government has had to repay either by a mortgage on the social development of the next generation, or by desperate measures of repudiation through inflation in its own generation. Either leads to devastating invasions of Liberty.

We may further amplify some of the effects of Regimentation upon the forces motivating our economic system. I have discussed in a previous chapter how the American System takes account of the natural, the practical and only powerful instincts which move men to constructive action that humanity has been able to discover since civilization began.

These creative impulses cannot be animated by continued money manipulation. That does not produce goods. Such action has only one final witchery and that is, to undermine the confidence of men in the future safety of their savings and thus to stifle their enterprise in renewing and improving their plant and equipment, and thus to continue unemployment. Business cannot be made universally profitable by suppression of the anti-trust laws, for this artificial maintenance of marginal production at the expense of efficient production increases prices and thus restricts national consumption. The government cannot secure through taxes as much productive capital as free thrift and saving would accumulate. The nation cannot add to its wealth by the dissipation of its savings through wasteful and non-productive government expenditures. It adds only poverty. Bureaucracy cannot replace the judgment of millions of individuals striving in their own interest. The government cannot compel energy and enterprise upon which productive power rests.

EFFECT OF MIXTURE OF SOCIAL SYSTEMS

The whole effect of bureaucratic direction and its interference, with its obvious conflicts, delays, confusions, and limitations, is to reduce productivity and consumption. Its result is not to stimulate men to effort but to hobble their initiative and activities. Whatever its maladjustments, the American System has through its creative impulses produced us a "plenty" unparalleled in history. In the deadening of these impulses by continued regimentation, our productivity cannot be sustained and we shall sink from an economy of plenty to an economy of scarcity.

SHOCKS UPON REPRESENTATIVE GOVERNMENT

The greatest shock of Regimentation, Fascism, Socialism, and Communism is upon Representative Government. The whole fabric of popular election, of separation of executive, legislative, and judicial powers, and of separation of national and local responsibilities, is integral in the American System. No one will doubt that pure Fascism and Communism can only exist under the abolition of every vestige of democracy. This illusion is that the institutions of popular government will not become mere ghosts under continuation of even partial Regimentation or government ownership and operation of competitive business. We should examine this illusion with care, for a destruction or weakening of the vitality of the protections of our liberties is the sure highway to destruction of Liberty itself.

REGIMENTATION'S EVASION OF THE SPIRIT OF THE CONSTITUTION AND OF ITS SAFEGUARDS

The encroachments upon our liberties may not be overt—by repeal of any of the Constitutional guarantees—but they may be insidious and no less potent through encroachment upon the checks and balances which make its security. More particularly does the weakening of the legislative arm lead to encroachment by the executive upon the legislative and judicial functions, and inevitably that encroachment is upon individual liberty.

If we examine the fate of wrecked republics over the world we shall find first a weakening of the legislative arm. Herein lay the decay of Continental European Liberalism. The lack of adequate cohesion among the members of these legislative bodies, the disintegration into blocs, the futility of discussions and negative action which was the inseparable result, so aroused resentment of the people that they turned them out for despotism and "action." It is in the legislative halls that Liberty commits suicide, although legislative bodies usually succeed in maintaining their forms. For 200 years the Roman Senate continued as a scene of social distinction and noisy prattle after it had surrendered its responsibilities and the Roman State had become a tyranny.

If we study our own legislatures over these later years we witness some of the same forces and the same turning of the people toward the executive arm, with consequent encroachment upon the militant safeguard to Liberty—legislative independence. We have seen some of the same lack of political cohesion, the growth of indefinite blocs of business, farm, veteran, labor, silver, public works, socialist and what not. We have seen the potency of these groups upon legislation, the primaries, and the elections. With every extension of the government into economic life, these blocs become more and more influential. These weakening poisons have further reactions.

Thus one of the astonishing evidences of legislative weakening has been the surrender of the parliamentary principle that the control of the purse was the surest check upon the Executive for which parliaments have fought and men have died over the centuries. In place of this hard-won legislative control we have now the curious idea that the Executive must protect the people from legislative endeavors to please group and sectional interests by huge and wasteful expenditures. It evidences an enormous surrender and shift of powers.

The difficulties of sustaining the balance of power between the executive and legislative arms, upon which the inviolability of Liberty depends, were thus great even without the impact of Regimentation.

The first result of this impact was evidenced after the legislation necessary to cure a banking panic, in that a host of bills affecting the whole future of the country, giving unprecedented powers to the Executive, were drafted outside the Halls of Congress, presented and enacted with scarcely any debate and no opportunity for public opinion to express itself. These surrenders of legislative responsibility will lower respect for the weight of the legislative arm in representative government which will last a generation, even if they have no worse effects. The acts of the recent months may be a passing eclipse of representative government, but a further examination of the consequences of continued Regimentation will show the inevitable increase of atrophy in the legislative arm.

Regimentation leads inexorably to an extension of bureaucratic politics in the election of members of the Congress. That all bureaucracy, old and new, must move and have its being in politics to maintain itself is evident. That it will as in the past—and with infinitely increased potency—constantly interfere in the choice of elected officials, including members of the Congress, needs no demonstration to those who know something of public life.

By the side of all this, Regimentation has already organized some four hundred trades and industries with their officially recognized representatives in the Capital. These representatives are made effective in influence upon government by the cloak of government agency. Their 1,500,000 different business firms are in every town and village, and each of them has potentially more than one vote. The interests of these regiments run parallel in many directions. Sooner or later their political good-will becomes necessary to every elected person. Thus we have organized invisible government into a smoothly oiled machine. Congress cannot run business but business can run Congress—to bankruptcy of Liberty.

Another process withering to representative government is the reaction upon a free legislative body of these enormously extended governmental activities. This becomes evident if we penetrate into a few details of this relationship. Any program of government, no matter how laudable or beneficial its aim, to change the habits or extend direction over the daily activities of the people must, perforce, adversely affect the interests of some of them. And the things here in action cannot be accomplished without many injustices, infinite hardships, deprivals of property and livelihood. Its sponsors believe these sacrifices must be made. We have a people highly sympathetic with those who thus suffer, for they are still much indurated with their old-fashioned ideas of justice, personal liberty, and rights. When great changes are proposed as temporary measures, such hardships will be borne with patience. When these same changes are developed as permanent new forms of government, even though they may seem attractive to a majority, yet encroaching upon centuries of heritage of personal liberty they will not be received by the minority without protest. Such resistance will rise from a host of the constituents to each member of the Congress and their appeal is at once to him or to the press.

Regimentation has already produced a factory of prayer-wheels directed at members of the Congress. Every one of millions of transactions by the government is at once selfish interest to the constitutents of some member. Every group interest, every sectional and group protest, every failure in working instantly reflects itself in demands upon him. Thus the legislative arm becomes at once entangled in a vast complex of interferences in the administration, out of which the member may win or lose votes at home.

In all this welter of pushing and pulling of the administrative bureaucracy by members of the Congress, the inescapable criticism and investigations from the Congress, the log-rolling and politics, no administrative machine can function properly. As a result, the Executive must sidetrack the legislative arm if administration of such a gigantic complex is to be effective. Either a free Congress will sooner or later destroy the ability of the system to function, or the system will destroy the freedom of the Congress.

In any case, the existence of a legislative body in a government which is operating competitive business or

"National Planning" or "National Regimentation" created an irreconcilable conflict reaching deep into the fundamentals of Liberty. That is the contradiction of a representative government the very purpose and function of which is to protect the unalienable rights of men, and a state where man has no rights or only part-time rights.

It is not my purpose to discuss the constitutionality of the many measures and acts upon which National Regimentation has been based. Whatever that situation may be, to adhere to the spirit of the Constitution and its safeguards, including orderly amendment, is the shelter of American life. To move away from these safeguards endangers the whole future of the philosophy of Liberty and thus the whole future of America. On that road one mis-step leads to another and then another until primary liberties are gone.

We have already noted many examples of the violation by Regimentation of the spirit and philosophy of Liberty. We may add further particulars which indicate where continuance of such a system will lead. They include instances of refusal of the right of men accused of wrong to be heard by independent tribunal; the cancellation of contracts with the government without any semblance of the processes of law; refusal or circumvention of the protection of the courts to citizens seeking redress from the government's own infringement of Constitutional rights; vesting of taxing powers in executive officials; the prosecutions of men for selling goods and services at less than their competitors; the coercion of merchants and manufactures into accepting the "Blue Eagle," and the instances of subsequent withdrawal of it to the ruin of their business by administrative officials, and that without any processes of the courts; the set-up of machinery which in effect dictates what manufacturers and farmers may produce and sell; the coercion of men to sign the codes and then the denial of them of their Constitutional protections from administrative action on the grounds that they had contracted these protections away to the government; the coercions of the people to sell a commodity—gold—to the government for less than it was worth, by denial of an open market and by threats; the whole business of devaluing every insurance policy and every savings bank deposit; the surrender by the Congress of its most serious responsibility for taxes and expenditures; and the whole invasion of the legislative responsibility, thus weakening the basic safeguards of Liberty. All this, and much more that could be recounted, indicate the way Regimentation invades the spirit if not the letter of the Constitution and becomes a transformation of government to the point where the citizen is entirely subjective to the state.

EFFECT UPON LOCAL GOVERNMENT

The whole process of Regimentation with its enormous extension of authority and its centralization in the Federal Government grievously undermines the State jurisdiction over its citizens; State responsibility, and in the end State's Rights. It thereby undermines one of the primary safeguards of Liberty. The failure of a minority of States to enforce laws which prevent an abuse of Liberty in employment of children, sweating of labor, manipulation of public markets, bad banking, and such, either compels or gives excuse to Federal invasion of State functions. But aside from any question of necessity in these particulars, with their penalties of remote controls less adapted to local needs, the extension of the Federal government into the dictation and operation of business, into direct relief, at once destroys some local responsibility, weakens some part of local self-government, and yields further and further opportunities for partisan political action, and brings some new infringement upon Liberty.

CLASS-CONFLICTS

One of the greatest achievements of America has been the repression of the growth of class-distinctions. To cast the nation into the trenches of class conflict, artificially stimulated by government regimentation and propaganda, is to stifle the very impulses to progress. The camps engage in struggle for self-preservation, and in this struggle the true interests of the nation are lost in the battles for self-interest with all their destructive consequences. That generates more and more repression.

The attempt to impose a forced system upon a people who have the traditions of generations of freedom drives a wedge through the heart of the whole nation. Whereas, under true Liberty, men are divided on ways and means for its fruition, under the attempt to impose forced economic life they must divide on the most fundamental principle of all—Liberty or government domination. Thus the nation is divided upon the issue which stirs most deeply the emotions of men.

EFFECT UPON FREE SPEECH AND FREE PRESS

Civilization has advanced only whenever and wherever the critical faculty in the people at large has been free, alive, and unpolluted. It slumps whenever this is intimidated or suppressed. That is the most certain lesson of history. This shift of human liberties by placing the government into business and agriculture, whether by operation or dictation, will be repulsive to the instincts of millions of people, and the government, in order to protect itself from the political consequences of its actions, is driven irresistibly and without peace to a greater and greater control of the nation's thinking.

Bureaucracy has already developed a vast ramifying propaganda subtly designed to control thought and opinion. The constant use of the radio, the platform, and the press, by device of exposition, news and attack with one point of view, becomes a powerful force in transforming the nation's mentality and in destroying its independent judgement. Bureaucracy's instinctive defense to criticism is to color the information and news with its objectives rather than presenting a cold analysis of results. It goes further in resentment to criticism and attempts to meet it with denunciation. We witness this vituperative impatience from those who believe they are serving the common good. Critics are smeared by personal attack upon character or motives, not answered by sober argument. Managed opinion is as much a part of "Managed Economy," as "Managed Currency," or as "Managed Agriculture." All this is the back door to repression of free thought and opinion. Free speech and free press have never lived long after free industry and commerce have been repressed.

No greater commentary is possible upon the whole question of free press or the invasion of Constitutional protections than the amazing contract insisted upon by the organized proprietors of newspapers with the Executive for a confirmation of the Constitutional guaranties of free press. That is unique in our history.

If we needed any further evidence of the consequences of continued Planned Economy or Regimentation upon our whole economic or governmental system, we may find it in the statement of one of its leading American advocates who is under no illusions. He says:

> It is in other words a logical impossibility to have a planned economy and to have business operating its industries, just as it is also impossible to have one within our present constitutional and statutory structure. Modifications in both, so serious as to mean destruction and rebeginning, are required."

Chapter 8

The Constructive Methods and Dynamics of Liberty

PURPOSE OF AMERICAN LIFE

The purpose of our American System is the betterment of the lives of men and women, through their economic security, the enlargement of their opportunities, and their intellectual, moral, and spiritual well being. The glory of America is that it has held this vision for all the people. The constructive purpose of this examination is to show the sole road by which these immense objectives can be attained.

CONSTRUCTIVE CRITICISM NECESSARY

In previous chapters we have examined the foundations, the growth, the utility, the ideals, and the accomplishments of the American System. We have shortly reviewed the current forms of foreign social philosophies and their economic organization. We have examined the social, economic, and governmental results and the ultimate consequences of National Regimentation, which embraces some of the elements of those foreign systems. We have seen that Liberty and these alien philosophies are incompatible systems. But constructive criticism cannot rest here. It requires the examination of the method for solution of the problems which confront us and the vitality of our system of Liberty to solve them.

I have stated that the Great Depression exposed great misuses of Liberty in our system; that we received great wounds from the aftermaths of the War; that we are faced with further great problems which are the product of our own free spirit of invention and progress.

REGENERATION OF THE SYSTEM OF LIBERTY

The choice before us is not that in rejection of Regimentation, Fascism, Socialism, or Communism we accept these abuses of Liberty or that we have less surety in the cure of these wounds and the solution of these problems. The real alternative before us and the real hope of humanity is to regenerate our system of Liberty, which has given so epic an achievement of human welfare in the past; that we purify its abuses; that we correct its weaknesses; that we free the dynamic impulses that cure its wounds and that daily invigorate its strength to solve our problems.

I shall therefore survey first some general aspects of our difficulties and the dynamic forces which assure progress through Liberty. Then for test and illustration of constructive methods under Liberty I shall shortly discuss the abuses which have gone within it. And I shall examine some larger problems which confront us and the alternative effect of other systems in their solution. I shall not enter upon the bypaths of detailed programs of national action, for the transcendent question before our people must be the system under which we shall live.

ECONOMIC PROBLEMS

While all our social and economic and governmental gears are deeply enmeshed, yet at this time economic adjustments overshadow the others. Our great international problems are mostly economic. The maintenance of democratic institutions depends mainly upon economic solutions. Our great social problems are to be solved largely through economic means. And the rapid growth of the sense of social responsibility over a half century brings all these solutions straight up to one purpose—betterment of all people.

Merely to enumerate some of the problems before us indicates their formidable character. The misuse of Liberty and economic dominations within its borders; the elimination of booms and depressions; technological unemployment; the increase in standards of living which will absorb the men released by labor-saving devices; the shifts in weight of debt; the undue proportion of national income at times invested in durable goods; the just distribution of income and wealth; the disparity of income between agriculture and industry; the constructive cure of poverty; the increased security of living; monetary and fiscal policies; international trade and exchange—these are but part of them and they are all concerned with human benefits.

Our difficulties appear far more forbidding when our problems are viewed in the mass than when dissolved into their individual parts. Some of them lose their importance when they are tested with facts and separated from emotions. Especially are they forbidding if we forget that many of them are marginal problems on branches of a system which otherwise functions to great advantage to all the people. Others indicate the primary needs of our times.

In considering long-view problems, except for emphasis, it is unnecessary to relate that our industrial civilization has traveled a long way from the primitive agricultural state where our forefathers laid down the principles of Liberty. The increase in families in a single century from half a dozen million to two dozen million requires of itself much cooperation to keep them from jabbing elbows. With the whole industrial development the invisible forces of economic life are far more potent and proceed with infinitely greater speed. The doings of some unknown speculator in New York or Chicago or San Francisco may have serious consequences in a thousand homes throughout the land. Remote events in other parts of the world affect the welfare of a million American farms. The cotton mill employing child labor inflicts great injuries at home and reverberates upon another community where thousands are thrust out of employment from inability to compete. The march of science and invention is constantly toward larger economic instruments and, with all their blessings, they offer new methods and new opportunities for wickedness and economic oppression.

DISTORTION OF OUR PROBLEMS

Our problems today are all strongly silhouetted against the background of depression. In the shadows of unemployment and misery of agriculture and business, causes are confused with effects. We dwell greatly upon the abuses and weaknesses of our system, exaggerating them out of all proportion. We at times overrate and at times underrate the powers of government in solutions. Emphasis is more often given to the emotional or the spectacular rather than the real. We fail to distinguish the fundamental from the superficial.

Short cuts are taken which lead to the bog. And from all this maze of problems and emotions many thoughtful people assume that our difficulties are due to an irreconcilable conflict of Liberty with our complex Industrial Age, that the free human spirit which created this modern civilization has made its own Frankenstein monster.

We must not conclude that ours is the only generation which has thought this, nor the first that has had to meet great perplexities. Men of every generation have envisaged their problems in terms of despair, but the dynamic impulses given to men from Liberty always have found tolerable solutions, so tolerable that a gigantic progress swept onward from generation to generation. If we would find the solutions for our problems, we cannot blink at the extent of our difficulties, nor underrate the resolute, unafraid, and enterprising spirit by which they must be met. But this spirit is alone the quality of men and women reduced to dependency of thought and action by regimentation.

In the pressure of the times many people analyze our difficulties of today as if they were due to inherent and incurable defects in the economic system of Liberty. They greatly confuse as apparent defects the weaknesses of individuals which will appear in any system, or the many transitory inheritances of war and its emotional aftershocks. Our people demand violent action in the cure of economic wounds when in fact their cure should be like those of bodily wounds. They must often be cured by the building up of cells of the economic body under careful nursing and antiseptics, rather than by surgery or patent medicines. In Liberty alone do the economic cells have the motivation and stimulation to action; repression kills them. And we should distinguish between economic wounds and economic disease. And above all we must beware of economic hypochondriacs.

In weighing the utility and genius inherent in a system built upon Liberty to solve such problems, it is difficult at times to preserve a long-distance forward perspective and a patience with the movement of human forces. But the same fogs have arisen in every depression—to be largely dissipated by the rising sun of recovery. In any event, two things are certain: we could see these problems in their true proportions and determine remedies much more effectively after a measure of recovery. The taking of strong drugs for them while still suffering from economic wounds of the war aftermaths does not conduce to clarity of vision or to rapid recuperation.

READJUSTMENT AND REFORM

The continuous adjustment of our society to new forces introduced by advancing science, the unending battle against economic domination, all require constant reform and amendment of our laws if we are to preserve Liberty. The growing recognition of public responsibility in the advancement of general welfare requires new commitments of government. Reform and amendment of our methods requires experiment. But there is as much danger in haphazard, ill-considered experiment as in stubborn opposition to all corrective movement and change. Experiment must be based upon the tenets of Liberty and experience and not blind trial and error practiced upon Liberty itself.

BOUNDARIES OF GOVERNMENT

If we would maintain our system of Liberty we must obviously confine the activities of government within certain boundaries. We must find solution to our problems without encroachment upon the guaranteed liberties, we must find them without impairment of the checks and balances of their guarantees. And that includes the field of State and local responsibilities as well as the Federal division of powers.

For once we begin to dim and limit our system of Liberty, the secondary results of diminishing productivity and increasing avarice will immediately take command and bog down the whole social structure.

THE DYNAMIC FORCE OF LIBERTY

The challenge to us is that the purpose of American life cannot be accomplished by the methods of Liberty and within the frame of a government that cannot itself infringe upon Liberty. The advocates of Regimentation declare that the American System leads to chaos. In demanding dictation of economic life they assume that the system of Liberty has not the vitality, the flexibility, the spiritual drive, to cope with the practical problems of modern economic organizations; that we must stifle the individual impulses of ordered Liberty for wishful economic efficiency through bureaucratic dictation under a new system that is economic and political tyranny.

Indeed one of the most profound questions and a test of any society is whether it possesses regenerative forces within itself to work out its own solutions. The oldest answer of Liberalism to even benevolent dictatorship has been that such benevolence and its supposed efficiency are not continuous; that the even succession of genius does not occur; and that a free society which evolves its own correctives and contains its own dynamic forces within itself may be at times less "efficient" but is the only society assured of permanence. Also a free society makes character in men which cannot be attained in dependency upon government.

The dynamic forces which produce progress lie deep below the surface in those human impulses which flower only in freedom. It is alone through the release of these instincts and aspirations that men and women develop their capabilities to the utmost. It is certain that the national sum of this utmost far surpasses that lesser sum which is inevitable under the repressions and interferences of all other systems. It is alone freedom of thought, of speech, of press, and the right to organize that give life and effectiveness to protest and correction of oppression and abuse. Liberty offers this unchallenged foundation for a progressive social system.

A declared part of the philosophy of those who object to our American System is the notion that America has reached the end of the road of economic development—the end of the road of progress. We have been told that our industrial plant is built, that our last frontier has long since been reached, and that our task is now not discovery or necessarily the production of more goods, but the sober, less dramatic business of administering the resources and plants already in hand.

That is a false assumption, for the frontiers of science, invention, and the inspiration of human behavior are as yet but barely penetrated by men. When we concede that progress is ended we concede that hope and new opportunity have departed. That is the concept of a static nation. It is necessarily the philosophy of decadence. No society can become static, it must go forward or back. Every society even to hold its gains must look forward to betterment. Its face must be bright with hope as have been the faces of generations of Americans. No society will function without confidence in its future opportunities. To maintain hope both for society and for the individual is indeed the first need of the world.

And ours is an economic system which for its own stability demands new inventions and new discoveries. Otherwise it halts and falters with infinite miseries. We must have new articles and new services which absorb those workers released from constant perfecting of the methods of making the older articles and services. The new wants and desires which arise from new additions to the standard of living, the new purchasing power which comes from economy in producing the already established standards are the motors that urge the wheels of economic progress.

The promise of continuing progress Liberty answers not only with a proud record of accomplishment, but with a dynamic philosophy of life. There are vast continents awaiting us of thought, of research, of discovery, of industry, of human relations, potentially more prolific of human comfort and happiness than even the "Boundless West." But they can be conquered and applied to human service only by sustaining free men, free in spirit, free to enterprise, for such men alone discover the new continents of science and social thought and push back their frontiers. Free men pioneer and achieve in these regions; regimented men under bureaucratic dictation march listlessly, without confidence and hope.

FUTURE PROGRESS

If we would continue progress by maintaining those freedoms of which progress is born, we at once have also to solve in that same flux of freedoms the vast accumulation of problems, which the very complexity of modern civilization has brought upon us.

In putting forward the method of constructive solution of our difficulties it is not necessary to rely upon the generalizations I have stated, dominating as they are. We may also examine a few major problems which have the widest social implications to determine whether there is a method and vitality for their solution within these boundaries, or whether violations of Liberty offer the only hope of solution.

There are two great categories of these problems which like all social, economic, and governmental problems are much interwoven. The first is the abuses of Liberty from within and the second and broad problems which the Industrial Age and War have brought to civilization. We will deal first with the abuses of Liberty.

Chapter 9

The Abuses of Liberty

BETRAYALS OF TRUST

While human frailty and human ingenuity develop many sins against Liberty in many fields, it is the abuses in the economic field which have been our most serious problem for the past two generations. In this time the major battle of Liberty has been against nascent and sporadic, big and little economic tyrannies to which the greed and love of power in men incline, and which the opportunities of the Industrial Age have much diversified. Betrayal of trust, manipulation, monopoly, exploitation, improper influence upon government, and all the other manifestations of predatory greed are traitorous to the high purposes of American life.

ECONOMIC OPPRESSION

Liberty is not to be had or held without effort. Abuses will develop in any economic system. We should frankly acknowledge them. But we should examine them to determine whether they are marginal problems in a system otherwise sound, whether the dynamic forces of Liberty are equal to their cure, whether there are constructive methods for their control, and whether some other system of society offers a better solution.

The abuses of Liberty fall naturally into two separate groups. First is the betrayal of public and private trust by individuals, and second are the problems of economic exploitation and domination which arise in modern business organization.

We have had heart-breaking betrayals of trust both in public and private life, mostly through crime or through loopholes in the law. Equally wicked and less known are those who have operated to destroy business and values of securities that they might profit from the losses of the people.

Such betrayals are not alone stealing of money. They injure the most precious faith that has ever come to a people—faith in Liberty. They cannot be atoned for by restitution or punishment. The men who have been guilty of these betrayals have, by breaking down confidence in our institutions and our economic system, by prejudice, hate, and discouragement they brought to our people, by the furious impulse to insensate action they aroused, contributed more to the cause of Regimentation, Fascism, Socialism, and Communism in the United States than all the preachments of Mussolini, Hitler, Karl Marx, or Lenin. No one has a right to condone an atom of it; anyone of even feeble instincts of righteousness will condemn every particle of it.

Because for a time a gangster runs loose, we must not assume that crime prevails through the whole American people, nor that the law or national ideals of decency and honesty have ceased to function. It is equally untrue that the more cultivated gangsters in big business represent either the morals or the regard for law in the general conduct of the financial and industrial institutions of the country. Betrayals of trust are not a part of the American System. They are violations of it. It is individual men who violate laws and public rights. It is men and not institutions or the economic system that must be punished for betrayals of trust. As indignant as we should be at such events, and much as they represent a serious evil in American life, we should remember that these instances are exceptions and not the rule, else they would long since have destroyed the Republic. We must not forget the great evidence of character from the untold hundreds of men who have reduced themselves to poverty to protect those who had reposed trust in them.

Greed and dishonesty are not incidents solely of the American System. A multitude of current examples could be adduced to prove that they infect all other countries and all other forms of society. We should not be stampeded into the belief that the liberty of a whole people held over these years of our national life should be abandoned for punitive purposes. We do not need to burn down the house to kill the rats.

The effects of economic abuse, exploitation of labor and of the public, and other economic dominations are of vastly greater importance than the occasional betrayal of trust. They are largely correctable by economic organization and legal administration. Their greatest corrective effort however is devotion to the Sermon on the Mount.

THE VALUES OF COMPETITION

Competition is in a large measure the most effective and dependable check upon rapacity and a preventive of economic domination and tyranny. The abolition of competition would lead to the death of production and progress in economic life. Yet competition is open to marginal abuses which must be regulated. Common honesty is not universal; some groups will conspire to avoid competition; some competitive processes, while not dishonest, yet result in destructive action which oppresses labor and the public; and some industries, by their nature, are semi-monopolies, where reliance upon competition is an insufficient safeguard of the public interest. Beyond these are the financial manipulation of business agencies; vicious speculation in their capital stocks; exploitation of the investor; and improper interference by business in government. These multiplied by the opportunities of new invention, new industry, and new ingenuity produce new loopholes for oppression and limitation of equal opportunity. The most precious ideals of American life have at times been dreadfully abused.

Perverse initiative will not do. There is no Liberty if the initiative of men may be freely devoted to robbery and tyranny, no matter in what guise. But after all these activities are but a small part of the great field of human action where constructive and scrupulous endeavor produces the great movement of national life. The opponents of the American System cite these misuses of Liberty as if they were its overwhelming characteristics. That they are marginal problems can be demonstrated in a few sentences. The billions of daily transactions among our people are carried on in justifiable confidence in integrity and fairness, or the economic clock would stop. The oft-repeated statement that 200 proportions control 90 per cent of the nation's wealth diminishes on examination to the fact that all corporations in the country, outside of banking and insurance companies, hold 30 per cent of the national wealth. Of this about one-third are small enterprises. Of the whole figure of 30 per cent, about one-third are railroads and utilities whose profits or rates are regulated, and the balance are of the competitive category. These corporations are not a thing apart from the people for they are owned by somewhere between six and ten million families.

Economic abuses or tyrannies do not always spring from greed, though that is often enough their origin. They often arise from a desire for power. The man of feudal type of mind is often generous and honest with a tinge of benevolence in his tyrannies, convinced that his is the correct service to his fellow men. His legal defense and his excuse is usually his false interpretation that the right of property or power over property exceeds the other rights, protections, and duties of Liberty. Liberty denies that the right of private property can be used to invade other rights and the establishment of this fact has been one of the struggles between true Liberalism and "the public be damned" attitude. But to deny that property can be so used is not a denial of the right of property. It is a denial of the right to use it for oppression. This type of mind will become even more obnoxious and dangerous in the opportunities for grasp of power in other social systems.

THE BATTLES OF LIBERTY AND ECONOMIC OPPRESSION

That the spirit of Liberty has been awake and virile in opposition to all forms of economic oppression requires no more proof than mention of the agitations at different times over "The Railroad Octopus," "The Wheat Pit," "Money Power," "Robber Barons," "The Trusts," "Special Privilege," "Monopolies," "Big Business," "Power Trust," "Wall Street"—all of which have a tincture of demagoguery, but they indicate a live public emotion in expression of fear of oppression from the constantly developing instrumentalities of industry and commerce. Nor have these fears been without warrant.

In prosperous times our people refuse to act in vigilance over their rights, and wrong-doing is then obscured by success in enterprise. We are aroused to remedial action only by vivid exposure of wrong-doing, long after our wiser men have protested. Hidden abuses come to the surface in times of stress and strain, and our people, moved by proper indignation, are easily led to the belief that the American System is at fault, and then to destructive action. We then confuse the mere size of honesty conducted enterprise with oppression.

Economic tyrannies are much older than Liberty. Indeed, our liberties were part born in rebellion of our forefathers from such tyrannies, a list of which appears in the Declaration of Independence. If we survey our experience since, we find that within the American System we have acted inexorably—albeit at times slowly—either by the States or by the Federal Government to remedy economic oppression.

THE BOUNDARIES OF REGULATION

We have developed State and Federal regulation of competition through the anti-trust laws by which we compel competition. We have so greatly succeeded in maintaining competition that Regimentation now claims it is too vigorous and that it should be greatly reduced by law. In the semi-natural monopolies, we have developed the regulation of rates, services, or profits in canals, turnpikes, railroads, ferries, electric power, gas, water, telegraphs, telephones, radio, and others. We have regulated the businesses engaged in public trust such as banks, insurance companies, building and loan associations, and others. We have required purity and proper presentation of goods. We have established the protection of health, and conditions of labor of men, women, and children, we have insisted upon fair competitive action, and acted in a score of other directions. Such regulations must be periodically revised but the long history of these advances demonstrates that Democracy can remain master in its own house.

The movements in regulation have all been battle-grounds in the definition of the borders between Liberty and economic oppression. These borders are not always exact, but they are capable of discovery and reasonable determination.

In regulation there must be the minimum necessary to attain true public ends. That is sound economics as well as Liberty. Otherwise industry is frozen and its development stunted. In our regulating devices there must be a sharp separation of judicial from executive powers through a definition of what is required by specific statutory laws. And enforcement of these laws must be by a politically free judicial system in which there is full access to higher courts. The individual must know precisely what his obligations and securities are, and must have the full protection of the courts in their inviolability. Thus we hold to the preservation of a "government of laws and not of men"—the first bulwark of Liberty. Our increasing tendency over years has been to vest vital regulatory powers in executive officials or alternatively to subject some judicial commissions to effective executive control. That is a crack in the wall against political tyranny. It chills initiative and enterprise by uncertainty and subjects it to politics which is worse. But still worse, where judicial authority is held by executive officials, the threat of their executive authority leads the citizen to acquiesce in injustice.

There is another boundary between those necessary regulations defining and inhibiting wrong-doing with property and, on the other hand, the inevitable tyranny of the state when it directs and dictates to men how they shall use their property. That is the distinction between the state as a policing agency and bureaucracy as the manager of business. The essence of American Liberty is to assure men the secured right to every activity which does not trespass the rights of others. Regulation as to what men may not do must not be confused with regimentation of men into platoons under a governmental corporal. That is the whole distinction between men possessing rights which cannot be transgressed by the state, and men merely as pawns of the state.

In all regulation we have another and very practical problem—that is, in building wall against oppression, that we do not, in seeking to save all the foolish and to prevent all the possible permutations of sin, damage the contributions to progress by thousands of honest men.

In our economic system there are certain self-acting restraints upon domination and abuse. The first of these is, of course, competition. Another is intelligent self-interest. Mass production succeeds by increased buying power, and increased buying power arises from increased wages and salaries. Production and distribution succeed by confidence of the customers. And in these days customers are affected by the attitude of business concerns upon public questions and their attitude toward their employees as well as by the merit of their product, and do not hesitate to exercise their choice.

There has been a great growth of the sense of trusteeship to the nation in the responsibilities of corporate management.

That is not a universal solution but it is a contribution to our corporate problem. The fact of wide-spread public indignation at violations itself indicates the growing standards demanded. No amount of regulation can replace such a sense of responsibility and its growth will march with the growth of public conscience.

Another self-acting regulation is free cooperation, by which the balance of strength among the groups in the system is maintained. The cooperation among farmers in marketing, the cooperation of labor in collective bargaining, to meet the aggregated capital of employers, the great mutual insurances, the building and loan associations, and savings institutions, are instances.

And we have gone further. We have properly used the credit and leadership of the government to promote great cooperative purposes—the Federal Reserve Banks, the Federal Land Banks, the Federal Home Loan Banks, the Farm Cooperatives. Here again there must be defined the boundary where government steps over the fundamental rights of free men and into tyranny. To avoid this these organisms must be so devised that they are operated by and ultimately pass into the ownership of those groups for whose better cooperation they are created—with only such minor governmental regulation as secured fair play, but without dictation by government or politics.

Free cooperation is never the extinction of personal Liberty. It is a strengthening of equal opportunity.

PART PLAYED IN ABUSE BY FINANCIAL INSTITUTIONS

If we would search for the origins of our recent difficulties from abuse of Liberty, we will find that much of it is the by-product of booms and slumps, and that a large part will disappear when we have planed out those interruptions in economic life. We shall find also that these abuses do not lie in the actual operation of production and distribution system as much as in our financial system. Also, if we survey the evidence, we shall find that betrayals of trust have largely disappeared from the industrial and distribution field. They have appeared mostly in the financial and banking fields. The increasing growth of domination by financial agencies over the industrial and distribution agencies has led to abuses by exploitation and vicious speculation which are in no sense the fault of the industries themselves.

The financial and credit set-up should be merely a lubricant to the systems of production and distribution. It is not its function to dominate and direct these systems. Moreover, that it should be so badly organized, that the volume of credit, whether long or short term, should expand and shrink irrespective of the needs of production and distribution, that it should be the particular creator of emotional fear or optimism; that it should be diverted from essential use in production and distribution to manipulation or speculation; that its functions should be misdirected to wildcat promotion instead of construction; that its depositories should be insecure; that there should be betrayal of trust and exploitation-all this is intolerable.

For some time, as I have said, we have needed to revise the older laws covering State and Federal regulation of the banks, financial institutions, and public exchanges in order to correct these evils and insure an organization adapted to our modern needs. This field has been hitherto left very largely to the States. From the failure of the States to carry out their responsibilities, and the interdependence of these institutions across State lines, we are forced to new adjustments in regulation. Better systems of finance and banking, against which the people find no complaint, have been found possible in other countries without the abandonment of Liberty. It is possible in America.

We need revision and coordination of our State and Federal regulatory laws in many other directions—over railroads, electric power, and other semi-natural monopolies, over waste of our natural resources, and over destructive competition with produced child labor and sweatshops. I have discussed these questions and those of stimulated cooperation in public interest can be accomplished within the domain of Liberty and without imposition of dictation and regimentation.

THE VIRILITY OF LIBERTY TO OVERCOME ABUSE

The question is, can we keep down the abuse of Liberty through the methods and principles of the American System or must we sacrifice Liberty and resort to Regimentation or some other system of bureaucratic operation or dictation of business? Will anyone but revolutionists say that the government should take over and operate the business agencies of the country because of sporadic sin? Does anyone seriously doubt that we are capable, by regulation of power companies, railroads, and other industrial agencies, of assuring that they will perform their functions fairly? Does anyone believe that these problems of effective organization and regulation of mere banks are so insoluble that we must sacrifice the liberties of a free-born race?

The proposals of other systems are that these marginal abuses of Liberty from the right—which is business—are to be replaced by major abuses of Liberty from the left—which is Bureaucracy and Tyranny. If the government has not the capacity, through regulation, to accomplish the easier task of an umpire, surely it cannot direct or run the system itself. Men chosen by election for oratorical triumphs or selected by bureaucracy will on average be no more honest, far less competent, and much more oppressive to Liberty than merchants, bankers, and industrialists operating under the law.

The alternatives, National Regimentation, Fascism, Socialism, or Communism, lead only to bureaucratic tyranny. Within the domain of Liberty is the sole system in which the dynamic forces of freedom of expression can give life to opposition and effective correction to abuse, whether from business or from bureaucracy. There is no doubt that the weeds of economic abuse will grow in the garden of Liberty. The fertile soil of this garden also produces the fine blossoms of enterprise and invention. Evil as the weeds are, it is far better to expend the labor to extirpate them than to lose the whole garden through the blight of tyranny.

Chapter 10

Economic Stability and Security

Beyond the question of internal abuses, an inquiry into the constructive method of social and economic organization for the future should consider the vitality of the system of Liberty to improve stability in the economic system, security in individual living, to attain just distribution of national income, and to cultivate our relations with other nations.

THE GREAT DEPRESSION

The first problem in public mind is the recovery from this depression. It involves questions pertinent to this examination. In this light it may be asked: Is the Great Depression the product of the economic system of Liberty? Can this system furnish recovery from it?

WAR CAUSES

It is of course necessary to deny any war contribution to its causes if one is to justify the claim that this depression was due to incurable defects in the economic system and that, therefore, all business should be regimented under government dictation—which is nonsense.

The depth and violence of this depression were enormously increased by its war origins and the aftermaths of inflation. To blame the American System for the Great Depression is necessarily to blame it for the Great War. The depression was a step in the liquidation of the war, and that holocaust originated in the despotisms of Europe. We should remember that humanity never has devised, at any time or at any place, nor ever will devise, an economic, social, or political system which can pass uninjured through the ravages of war.

That other causes than war contributed to the Great Depression will readily be admitted, but the most terrific destructive impacts upon our economic system, already disorganized by our own inflation, by our own industries unbalanced by the war and by our own speculative madness, came in 1931 out of the war-caused financial collapse of the area of former despotisms of Central Europe. They came with such violent repercussions that even the "Planned Economy" of Fascism in Italy and of Socialism in Russia suffered equally with all other nations. Our economic system built on Liberty is a system designed for peace. If war for other than defense is to be our purpose, we may stop this discussion at this point and admit that some other system must be adopted at once.

RECOVERY IN 1932

Our system of Liberty proved its vitality to recover even from this particular and unusual depression just as it did from the great depression which followed the Civil War. The tremendous battle to prevent world economic chaos was fought concurrently in many countries in the summer and fall of 1931 and the winter and spring of 1932. The depth of the depression had been passed in the summer of 1932. The lifting effect of domestic and world measures and the natural forces of recovery became evident in every branch of national life during the summer and fall of 1932—as they did also in the sister democracies, the British Commonwealth, and France. Increases in employment, increasing prices in securities and commodities, all marked this turn of the tide.

SETBACKS IN 1933

Ours was the only country in which there was subsequent hesitation in this forward movement. The election by its determination of an abrupt change in national policies naturally brought a break in the march of confidence and recovery. This hesitation quickly transformed itself into alarm among an enlarging circle who were convinced that under the new policies the gold standard would be abandoned, that inflation and enormous government outlays and borrowing would be undertaken. These alarms resulted in vast withdrawals of gold, a flight of capital abroad, and runs upon banks, despite the solvency of the system as a whole, which quickly precipitated a banking panic. After the banks were reopened it was found that those which were declared sound covered only 92 per cent of the deposits in the country.

Recovery from this depression is inevitable, though it may be slowed up by government policies. The outstanding fact is, however, that two great Liberal nations, the United States and the British Commonwealth, demonstrably turned from the World Depression in the summer of 1932. I confidence were restored in the securities of Liberty we should move forward irresistibly.

BASIS OF ECONOMIC STABILITY

Economic stability is the first need for any system and indeed for the preservation of Liberty and the survival of civilization itself. The major disturbers to stability are wars, whether military wars or trade wars; unbalanced budgets, with their perpetual threat of inflation; unstable currencies; and booms and their recoil of depressions. I have already touched upon fiscal and currency methods in their dangers to Liberty.

BOOMS AND SLUMPS

The boom and slump are also in large degree within our control. These storms are marked by over-optimism, by inflation of credit or currency, overexpansion, overproduction, vicious speculation, waste and exploitation—followed by the inexorable liquidation of these indulgences, marked by exaggerated fears, deflation, stagnation, unemployment, losses to business and agriculture, bankruptcy, and infinite misery.

In solution of this problem lies a major contribution to a great area of associated problems, such as destructive competition, sweated labor, rapacious speculation, financial instability and exploitation, unemployment, and periodic overexpansion of industry, for they are all part of the same vicious cycle.

The ordinary cyclic movements of boom and slump can be greatly reduced in their effects. To assume that the ravages of speculation and the out-of-balance of production and consumption are wholly their cause is to confuse part of the origins of the disease with the symptoms.

Without entry into detail, our recent experience shows that we have not given sufficient weight to the tides of mass emotions of optimism and fear, both in their origination and their acceleration of the height and depth of these movements. If the human race had not been born optimistic, it would have committed suicide fifty centuries ago in the face of the difficulties that began with the dawn of civilization. And I may add that man is also an animal given to speculating upon his hopes under mass emotions. But he is equally subject to panics of fear which profoundly influence mass behavior in the opposite direction.

To indicate the importance of the part which these emotions play in our modern economy, I may cite that, in President Washington's time, the proportion of human labor devoted to the production and distribution of commodities not essential to bare food, clothing and shelter quite likely did not amount to more than a small percentage of the total. Today, we probably find more than half of our employment in the production and distribution of non-essentials, that is, goods and services other than the bare necessities of life. Whereas optimism and fear do not greatly affect consumption of essentials at any time, yet such non-essentials are enormously and instantly affected by boom and slump psychosis. Today, at the slightest appearance of over-optimism, the people concurrently increase their standards of living and their new enterprises with consequent acceleration of the consumption of non-essential goods. On the other hand, fear quickly causes restriction in living, a hesitation in enterprise, and an abrupt slowing down of the whole economic machine. Moreover, in the early days of the Republic, optimism or fear moved very slowly, because of the task of both communication and economic understanding. Today waves of hope, confidence, and fear spread almost instantaneously. The failure of a great bank in Vienna reverberates in San Francisco in an hour.

The consequence is that the modern ebb and flow of emotional tides become infinitely more accelerated and more devastating. And both optimism and fear feed upon themselves, for emotional men always strive to anticipate results. Fear alone often creates a very hurricane of destruction.

We have learned from this recent experience that the most dangerous impact of fear is upon the financial and credit structure, for that is the most sensitive and the most defenseless agency under attack by fear. Soundness of assets is no protection against a bank run. The appearance of fear in depositors at once affects the bankers, and with their curtailment of credit they further stifle production and consumption. Milder forms of fear may be only a check upon business activity, but in its violent form of banking panic it becomes paralysis.

The dominant accelerator of optimism and speculation is credit or currency inflation. We are thus brought again to the necessity for the establishment of a stable financial and credit system as the first major attack upon the vicious cycle of optimism and fear. That is, we require a system which will serve as a brake upon that optimism and inflation which create booms, with their speculative building or gambling, and will also be impregnable to destruction from the fear which accelerates depressions.

There are other elements which contribute to the periodic distortions and the unequal advance of industry.[14] Some are in part causes and in part effects and some are uncontrollable

---

[14]There is much current discussion over the contribution to instability of the effect of ill-balance between savings and expenditures on consumption goods, and the ratio of profits and wages. Irrespective of the merit of the thesis the emphasis upon these factors would be moderate if the exponents would spread before them the national balance sheet, determine the actual amounts that are involved, and bear in mind with less violent depressions the amounts involved in these factors are much less.

under any system, such as events in foreign countries, the effect of climatic and other periodic influences on production, and new and revolutionary inventions. Some are correctable. Some are the pains of growth, which we could accept with equanimity and deal with by prevention of suffering and better foundations of individual security.

But aside from the threat and consequences of war, and the effect of budget deficits and unstable currencies, when we have improved our financial organization we shall have solved the vicious acceleration of optimism and fear and thus greatly narrowed the violence of booms and depressions with their deserts of unemployment and agricultural misery. We shall then have eliminated a large part of the periodic ill-balance of production and consumption, and shall have removed much of the opportunity for exploitation and vicious speculation. All this is possible of achievement within a system built upon Liberty.

The cure of booms and slumps proposed by Regimentation, Fascism, and Socialism is that the government operate or dictate the economic system. But practical experience in the other countries under those systems does not show any evidence of either prevention or cure.

ECONOMIC SECURITY OF THE INDIVIDUAL

A larger part of social hope, economic thought and governmental action in our times is directed to the provision of greater individual security of life and living. It is by the allurements of instant solution of this fundamental human problem that all the new systems of society superficially commend themselves.

The American System envisages this problem as the abolition of poverty among those who have the will to work and thus the abolition of that haunting specter of humanity—the fear of dependency. Therein lies great freedom of spirit.

There has been—at least since our society realized that its new inventions enabled it to produce a plenty—a general acceptance of the responsibility that the system should provide a foundation of security to the deserving which would afford them economic safety and freedom from fear. And the gospel of Christ imposes upon us the duty to see that those who have suffered misfortune shall also be protected.

But the first requirement of solution is to sustain an economic system which has proved its ability to produce a "plenty" of goods, services, and comforts adequate for the needs of the whole population.

And again it can be said, and with emphasis, that there is no other system, whether it be Regimentation, Fascism, Socialism, or Communism, that does not slow down the human stimulus and thereby decrease the volume of production. Without this plenty we may as well stop talking about the problems of poverty and insecurity, for we will have nothing to talk about but insecurity and poverty, and those will become the sole source of our emotions.

ADVANCES MADE

Having secured the "plenty" and the constant forward movement of the standards of living are nine-tenths of the great battle of humanity against poverty. This victory imposes the duty of winning the remaining sectors. They lie today mainly in finding greater stability for employment and agriculture by straightening out the economic cycle, and finding systematic methods of positive individual security against the misfortunes of unemployment and sickness, and for assurance in old age.

The advances already made in economic security must not be overlooked. Security has been provided in education, public health, a vast area of medical treatment, wide ranges of recreation, care of orphans, pensions to the needy and the aged in many states, public pensions to government servants, to veterans, private pensions in educational institutions, hospitals, and many industries, and the assumption of responsibility by government to relieve distress from depression unemployment. A vast amount has been accomplished in providing the security which lies in independent home and farm ownership, in building up of insurance and savings. Also we should not ignore the indirect effect of powerful economic forces operating in our system, such as the spirit of maximum efficiency in American labor and agriculture; the incentives to spread consumption through low unit costs of production and profit and the highest possible wages; and the division of the available work. These are all no doubt contributory to profitable and stable business, but as they profoundly affect wider diffusion of national income they are just as surely aids to higher standards of security from poverty and dependency.

The difficulties of complete and empirical solution of the problem are not the denial of social responsibility to solve it. The difficulties are in discovery of methods which will not deteriorate thrift, create a group of loafers, and will not undermine the responsibilities of state and local government, or lay unjust burdens upon agriculture. The problem of assurance against undeserved poverty is soluble and it becomes increasingly clear that the true American System alone can solve it, for that system alone will produce the plenty. The complexity of this problem does not demand the surrender of Liberty. Instead its surrender will inevitably destroy our ability to produce the goods with which to provide the remedy.

WIDER DIFFUSION OF INCOME AND PROPERTY

There enters into the problem of security also the just division and diffusion[15] of the national product. That some individuals receive too little and some receive too much for the services they perform is a certainty. The contrast between poverty in a hard-working, thrifty home and the perverse extravagance of the willful drones is a blot. But we may point out that with the diffusion of income in normal times under our system among 25,000,000 American families, it cannot be justly claimed that more than a fringe of a few hundred thousand receive more than they deserve for the service they give the community and that there are not more than a few million on the other fringe who conscientiously work and strive and do not receive that to which they are justly entitled. In between lies the vast majority of our people.[16] Over the last half-century except for the interruption of depressions, our standard of living, which is

[15]I here use "diffusion" instead of "distribution," for that term so commonly connotes the purely business function of the delivery of goods.

[16]There has been spread a vast amount of misinformation upon the whole subject of diffusion of income and wealth. That is the natural method of those who are anxious to destroy liberty. A competent study will show that over 90 per cent of the national income goes to persons receiving less than $10,000 per annum income and over 97 per cent to persons receiving less than $50,000 annually. These individuals in the higher brackets pay from 30 to 60 per cent of their income away in taxes. A study of the distribution of national wealth shows that about 74 per cent belongs to persons of less than $10,000 per annum income and 89 per cent to persons receiving less than $50,000 annual income.

the real test of diffusion, has increased steadily and the proportion of families in the area of poverty has decreased constantly.

The constant ideal of the whole American System has been thrift and the wider and wider diffusion of property. That makes for solution of many social questions including the whole problem of security in rainy days and old age. But there can be no incentive to acquire such security unless the right to honest possession is maintained.

Distribution of national wealth and income must from any constructive point of view embrace the widest considerations of stimulation to effort. What the absolute gauge of payment for service may be which will stimulate work, initiative, and enterprise will never be completely determined on this earth, for there is no common currency between the several rewards for which men strive—whether they be money or power or mental or spiritual satisfactions. But society must have the maximum effective work, and to get it, men must be given competitive rewards which inspire labor and enterprise. We can better afford to pay too much for creative enterprise than too little, for creative activity brings reward to the whole nation.

The American System has long since realized the necessity of curbing the undue amassing and concentration of wealth. The denial of primogeniture, the constant drive to preserve competition, to control monopoly, the drastic taxes upon inheritance, all have shown evidence of this realization. A vast amount of so-called concentration of wealth for recent years is the concentration of "stage money" created by war and boom inflation; and in this aspect the Great Depression has been a most drastic agent in its redistribution.

Nothing is more certain than that we require a constantly wider diffusion of income. But this constantly wider diffusion which all thinking people desire comes slowly, for violent action distributes more poverty than wealth.

And one of the solutions of this problem lies in devoting our energies to recovering and increasing the total income and wealth of the nation, and thus having still more to diffuse. We build progress not upon static standards but upon expanding desires and a steadily forward movement of material and mental satisfactions. Therein is the nation free, moving, vibrant and alive with opportunity and security for our children.

SECURITY FROM MILITARY AND ECONOMIC WAR

Liberalism has been ever the exponent of peace among nations. It is the surest hope of peace. Not in a hundred years have the great democracies of the world gone to war with each other. Yet that same century has been splattered with blood from despotisms battling with each other, and from Liberal governments defending themselves against attacks by such nations. The most practical proposal of peace to the world has been the extension of self-government. Peoples are far less likely than authoritarian governments to start wars.

Modern despotism, in every case, has achieved its purpose by fanning the fires of Nationalism. To inflame hate, and to stir the sacred emotion of patriotism as a drug to liberty, is a favorite device of those who seek power. Their effect is to increase enormously the dangers of conflict.

Today the defensive complex of dictatorships seems to require that they attack Liberalism as the enemy of peace, at least with words. Such, for example, is Premier Mussolini's familiar statement that "the era of Liberalism, after having accumulated an infinity of Gordian knots, tried to untie them in the slaughter of the World War—and never has any religion demanded of its votaries such a monstrous sacrifice. Perhaps the Liberal gods were athirst for blood?"

From rather an extensive contact with the World War and its aftermath, I was under impression that it was started by certain despotisms in Central and Eastern Europe and that the Liberal civilizations were obliged to fight to preserve their liberties. That the Liberal nations failed in imposing much of their philosophy upon those former despotisms will be admitted, but it would seem a more just appraisal that the seeds of the Great War lay in despotism—not in Liberalism.

The destruction of democracies and the rise of despotisms since the war has largely destroyed the world efforts at organized peace and disarmament. The weakening of representative governments in Germany, Italy, Japan, and a number of Eastern European states has sensibly increased the dangers to peace. The increase in despotisms necessarily imposes a greater expenditure for preparedness upon democracies.

The rise of rampant Nationalism has resulted in great damage to the economic stability for the world. Moreover, the world heretofore in periods of depression has had relief through great movements of people to the unsettled lands and in emigration from one country to another. These are almost absent today. The constant perfection of the economic machine has given the world immensely greater productivity. Under this productivity, populations have hugely increased. In the absence of these older reliefs and in the presence of greater burdens, governments of necessity must take new and unprecedented measures of direct relief at a time when the people are least able to furnish them with such resources. The crisis is thus prolonged. And when governments as part of their relief have endeavored to stop imports and stimulate exports with the weapons of currency depreciation, they further prolong the crisis.

The world today, including ourselves, is engaged in a fierce trade war in which the chief weapons are tariffs, quotas, and other restrictions on imports, subsidies of exports, and militant currencies subsidized by taxpayers' monies through governmentally "stabilized" exchange. Until the use of this currency weapon is abandoned and the currencies of the chief commercial countries are stabilized by open agreement, there can be no effective relaxation in the increasing trade barriers of a hundred varieties. Until this be done the world's price levels, the market for surplus goods, and the world's business in general will continue to be chaotic.

If our civilization is to be perpetuated the great causes of world peace and world cooperation in economic life must prevail. These immense objectives to the welfare of all mankind can prevail only through cooperation among nations. No matter how great the domestic efforts in any nation may be for the betterment of its people, they will be checked and limited if they be founded upon any other concept.

The dangers and destruction to Liberty from war should need no demonstration after the experience of the last two decades. It should also be grasped that economic war inevitably drives to further centralization of power in government and is equally perilous to Liberty, for in these operations are found daily new plausible reasons fir more and more dictation of domestic economic life.

In thus outlining the method of solution of some major social and economic problems I do not wish it assumed that these comprise the whole range of them. To review them all would dissipate into many bypaths the purpose of this examination. That is to demonstrate the constructive method of solution of our problems under the system of Liberty and the destructive method of its alternatives. We have great problems in maintaining representative government, in law enforcement, and in dealing with crime. The problems of home life, of home ownership, of city concentration, of rural life, of education, of recreation, of moral and spiritual advancement are live in national consciousness. The extent and nature of our complexities, yet but partly solved, are outlines in detail by the Committee on Recent Social Trends. That the ferment of national organizations is at work in every village, city, and state, stimulating discussion, pursuit, and solution, is itself the proof of the vigor of our system. Such inquiries and organizations are the offspring solely of free men. Their very existence is demonstration not alone that there is no lack of will, but that the will rises from the great mass of our people. It is a will to find progress by their own efforts. That is the product of a free people, not a people directed by bureaucracy.

In final analysis the question which we have to meet in solution of all of these problems is: Having a system which has given history a record of greater security and comfort to a greater number than ever in all human history before; having without sacrifice of Liberty solved our dangers time and again; having the capacity, the will, and the method to keep solving them, shall we now surrender to follow paths which can lead only to deadened inspirations and abandoned freedoms?

In the methods of Liberty there is a vast constructive program before us. If we maintain its dynamic forces of life, if we strive for peace, if our economic system be cleared so far as humanly possible of abuse, if we develop the stability which is obviously attainable, if we advance personal security, then with vigilance in our moral and social responsibilities, the other many problems of the times will find the solutions.

Chapter 11

We May Sum Up

The issue of civilization today is whether Liberty can survive the wounds it has received in these recent years.

LIBERALISM AFTER THE WAR

After the war, Liberalism came into a vast ascendency. The arms of democracy had been victorious over the legions of despotism. Those dismembered nations hastened with high hopes to adopt the forms and endeavored to develop the spirit of individual Liberty.. Then came the dreadful aftermaths—the vengeance peace, the continuation of hate, the realization of losses from the gigantic destruction, the rise of bitter nationalism with all its barriers and snatching for advantage, the attempts by inflations to shift and postpone the debt burdens of the day, the vicious speculation and exploitation to which inflation gives opportunity, the dislocations from rapid advances of scientific discovery and labor saving devices, and the final plunge into the liquidation by the great depression. The Human misery that has flowed from it all has discredited the social systems of all nations, no matter how great their concept of liberty, justice, and peace.

Liberalism fell first in its new-born regions, and today it is under attack in the great areas of its origins and development. Indeed, the fate of Liberalism rests today mainly upon three great nations, America, the British Commonwealth, and France. It is within these areas where the fortresses of freedom though much weakened can be held. If they fail the lesser outerworks will fall. In America, where Liberty blazed brightest and by its glow shed light to all others, it is today impaired and endangered.

EFFECT OF ALTERNATE PHILOSOPHIES

In the anxiety and hope, in the yearnings of humanity for betterment, alternative philosophies of society have sprung into life, offer "solutions" for all difficulties. Whatever their names—Fascism, Socialism, or Communism—they have this common result: wherever these systems have been imposed tyranny has been erected, government by the people abolished. The protection of law has vanished before dictation; no person is secure in justice; even the old right of *habeas corpus* is forgotten; the right of property is wholly removed or its use permitted only upon sufferance by the state; free speech, free press, the right of assembly have been banished; whispers and terror replace security and freedom of spirit. From these repressive measures come the banishment of freedom itself.

Be it noted that even "temporary" dictatorships are achieved by the direct and emphatic promise to the people that their liberties eventually will be restored. In Russia, the theory runs that some liberty will be restored when the revolution of the proletariat is "consummated." In Italy, liberties will be restored as the people earn them by faithful obeisance before the throne of Fascism. Under Naziism, liberties will be restored when the "National Consolidation" is secured.

A sobering commentary upon the processes of mass psychology is the idea in all of these countries that Liberty may be achieved and secured only by sacrifice of liberties to the efficiency of tyranny. Certainly it is not illogical to suggest that if the ultimate purpose of dictatorships is the restoration of Liberty, the first aim of existing liberal governments should be the defense and maintenance of Liberty.

The proponents of these rival programs are often men of burning zeal. In their zeal they are willing to wipe out centuries of achievement, to ignore the bloody road over which the human race has travelled, evolving as it went the very ideals of justice and liberty. They envisage these ideals as their own and sole discovery, they adopt actions and measures which this long road of trial has proved disastrous, and they abandon the gains of freedom so painfully acquired.

From the examples of National Regimentation that we have examined it is obvious that many of its measures represent not reform or relief within the boundaries of Liberty, but that they are emulating parts of some of these other systems with the hope of speeding recovery from the depression.

One may disagree and keep silent as to the justification of some of these measures if they are to be limited to "emergency," for in the march of a great people that is relatively unimportant if that is all of it. Then these dangers and stresses will disappear as an eddy in the stream of national life. The important thing is whether this drift from essential liberties is to be permanent. If not permanent, these emergency measures will have served the purpose of having exhausted the pent-up panaceas of a generation and broken them on the wheel of resistant human behavior and the spirit of a people with a heritage of liberty.

EFFECT OF PERMANENT NATIONAL REGIMENTATION

The threat of the continuance of these "emergency" acts is a threat to join the Continental retreat of human progress backward through the long corridor of time. In the demands for continuance there lies a mixture of desperate seeking for justification of their adoption and subtle ambitions of those advocating other philosophies. Whatever the motive, the promise of permanence now stares the American people starkly in the face. It is not the mere evolution of an economic procedure that this Regimentation implies—it steps off the solid highways of true American Liberty into the dangerous quicksands of government dictation.

Thus, what I am interested in in this inquiry is something that transcends the transitory actions, as important as they are, something far more pregnant with disaster to all that America has been to its people and to the world. No nation can introduce a new social philosophy or a new culture alien to its growth without moral and spiritual chaos. I am anxious for the future of freedom and liberty of men. That America has stood for; that has created her greatness; that is all the future holds that is worth while.

IMPORTANCE OF THE CHOICE BEFORE US

The unit of American life is the family and the home. Through it vibrates every hope of the future. It is the economic unit as well as the moral and spiritual unit. But it is more than this. It is the beginning of self-government. It is the throne of our highest ideals. It is the center of the spiritual energy of our people.

The purpose of American life is the constant betterment of all these homes. If we sustain that purpose every individual may have the vision of decent and improving life. That vision is the urge of America. It creates the buoyant spirit of our country. The inspiring hope of every real American is for an enlarged opportunity for his children. The obligation of our generation to them is to pass on the heritage of Liberty which was entrusted to us. To secure the blessings of Liberty to ourselves and to our posterity was the purpose in the sacrifice of our fathers. We have no right to load upon our children unnecessary debts from our follies or to force them to meet life in regimented forms which limit their self-expression, their opportunities, their achievements. St. Paul said nearly two thousand years ago, "Ye have been called unto liberty."

THE BILL OF RIGHTS

Our American System and its great purpose are builded upon the positive conception that "men are endowed by their Creator with certain unalienable Rights, that among these are Life, Liberty, and the pursuit of Happiness;" that the purpose and structure of government is to protect these rights; that upon them the government itself has come that unloosing of creative instincts and aspirations which have builded this, the greatest nation of all time.

The Bill of Rights—our forefathers' listing of unalienable liberties and personal securities—was written a century and a half ago. We have had need to work out practical application of these liberties and the machinery for maintaining them in the changing scene of the years. We have seen some of them fade from memory, such as the protection from quartering of troops. We have had to add some new rights to assure freedom from slavery and to give universal franchise. We have had to keep the balance as between some of them and to see that some—chiefly property rights—are not used to override other rights. We have steadily developed from the spirit of freedom high standards and ideals of human relationship, a great system of advancement of mankind. We have at times failed to live up to our ideals, but that they shall continue to shine brightly is the important thing.

Those are today denounced who, on one hand, dare assert that these liberties and personal securities still live, and, on the other, they are equally denounced who assert that they have been transgressed. It will be denied that any one of them has ever been mentioned in our country for repeal or modification. Nor has it been proposed today that any new rights and securities should be added to those guaranteed by the Constitution. Therein lies the intellectual dishonesty of the attack upon them. If we have discovered that any one of these liberties is not our individual endowment by the Creator, the right thing is to propose a change in the Constitution and allow us to examine it, not to extinguish it by indirection. Such an alteration would not get far, for whether people know them by name or not, the principles of liberty and security are embedded in their daily thought and action. Perhaps not one in a hundred thousand of our people knows the detailed list of liberties our forefathers insisted upon, or the development of them since, but never a day goes by that every man and woman does not instinctively rely upon these liberties.

Yet today forces have come into action from ignorance, panic, or design which, either by subtle encroachment or by the breaking down of their safeguards, do endanger their primary purpose. These liberties are of urgent practical importance. The very employment upon which millions depend for their bread is today delayed because of the disturbance of confidence in their security.

ITS ENEMIES

There are those who assert that revolution has swept the United States. That is not true. But there are some who are trying to bring it about. At least they are following the vocal technique which has led elsewhere to the tragedy of Liberty. Their slogans; their promise of Utopia; their denunciation of individual wickedness as if these were the wards of Liberty; their misrepresentation of deep-seated causes; their will to destruction of confidence and consequent disorganization in order to justify action; their stirring of class feeling and hatred; their will to clip and atrophy the legislative arm; their resentment of criticism; their chatter of boycott, of threat and of force—all are typical enough of the methods of more violent action.

In our blind groping we have stumbled into philosophies which lead to the surrender of freedom. The proposals before our country do not necessarily lead to the European forms of Fascism, of Socialism, or of Communism, but they certainly lead definitely from the path of liberty. The danger lies in the tested human experience, that a step away from liberty itself impels a second step, a second compels a third. The appetite for it, and power over the rights of men leads not to humility but to arrogance, and arrogance incessantly demands more power. A few steps so dislocate social forces that some form of despotism becomes inevitable and Liberty dies.

EFFECTS OF EVEN PARTIAL REGIMENTATION

No country or no society can be conducted by partly acknowledging the securities of Liberty and partly denying them, nor by recognizing some of them and denying others. That is part democracy and part tyranny. At once there are conflicts and interferences which not only damage the whole economic mechanism but drive unceasingly for more and more dictation.

Even partial regimentation cannot be made to work and still maintain live democratic institutions. Representative government will sooner or later be at conflict with it along the whole front, both in the incidentals of daily working and in the whole field of free choice by the people. If it be continued the Congress must further surrender its checks and balances on administration and its free criticism since these, with intensified duties to its constituents, create interferences that will make efficient administration of this regimented machine impossible.

For any plan of Regimentation to succeed it must have not only powers of rigid discipline but adamant continuity. Does anyone believe that with the interferences of the Congress and the storms of a free press any government can impose discipline and follow a consistent and undeviating course in directing the activities of 125,000,000 highly diversified people? Because such a course is impossible Fascism and Sovietism have suppressed both free speech and representative government.

PROTECTIONS OF LIBERTY

We are confronted with a maze of problems. The boom and depression brought discouraging increases and disclosures of the abuses of Liberty and the growth of economic oppressions. I have discussed these abuses at length in previous chapters because these betrayals of trust, exploitation, monopoly, and all the rest of them are the battle-grounds of Liberty.

The American System has steadily evolved the protection of Liberty. In the early days of road traffic we secured a respect for liberties of others by standards of decency and courtesy in conduct between neighbors. But with the crowding of highways and streets we have invented Stop and Go signals which apply to everybody alike, in order to maintain the same ordered Liberty. But traffic signals are not a sacrifice of Liberty, they are the preservation of it. Under them each citizen moves more swiftly to his own individual purpose and attainment. That is a far different thing from the corner policeman being given the right to determine whether the citizen's mission warrants his passing and whether he is competent to execute it, and then telling him which way he should go, whether he likes it or not. That is the whole distance between ordered Liberty and Regimentation.

ACHIEVEMENT OF A "PLENTY"

The achievements of our own economic system have brought us new problems in stability in business, in agriculture, and in employment, and greater security of living. But the first constructive step in solution is the preservation of Liberty, for in that sphere alone are the dynamic forces with which to solve our problems successfully.

The whole history of humanity has been a struggle against famine and want. Within less than half a century the American System has achieved a triumph in this age-long struggle by producing a plenty.

The other systems now urged for permanent adoption propose to solve the remaining problem of distribution of a hard-won plenty by restrictions which will abolish the plenty. To adopt this course would be an abject surrender. Worse, it would be a surrender to the complexities of distribution after the major battle, which is production, has been won. It may be repeated that if we undermine the stimulants to individual effort which come alone from the spirit of Liberty, we may well cease to discuss the greater "diffusion of income," "of wealth," "minimum standards," and "economic security," the "abolition of poverty," and its fears. Those are possibilities only in an economy of plenty.

NATIONAL REGIMENTATION A RETROGRESSION

It is not that the proposals or philosophies or tendencies of National Regimentation are new discoveries to humanity, which offer the bright hope of new invention or new genius in human leadership. They have the common characteristic of these other philosophies of society and of those of the Middle Ages—that the liberties of men flow only from the state; that men shall be regimented, not free men. Herein is the flat conflict with true Liberalism. It is all old, very, very old, the idea that the good of men arises from the direction of centralized executive power, whether it be exercised through bureaucracies, mild dictatorships or despotisms, monarchies or autocracies. For Liberty is the emancipation of men from power and servitude and the substitution of freedom for force of government.

LIBERTY IN THE MACHINE AGE

Liberty comes alone and lives alone where the hard-won rights of men are held unalienable, where governments themselves may not infringe, where governments are indeed by the mechanisms to protect and sustain these liberties from encroachment. It was this for which our fathers died, it was this heritage they gave to us. It was not the provisions with regard to interstate commerce or the determination of weights and measures or coinage, for which the Constitution was devised—it was the guaranties that men possessed fundamental liberties apart from the state, that they were not the pawns but the masters of the state. It has not been for the aid and comfort of any form of economic domination that our liberties have been hallowed by sacrifice. It has not been for the comfort of machinery that we have builded and extended these liberties, but for the independence and comfort of homes.

Those who proclaim that in a Machine Age there is created an irreconcilable conflict in which liberty cannot survive should not forget the battles of liberty over the centuries, for let it be remembered that in the end both big business and machinery will vanish before freedom if that be necessary. But it is not necessary. It is not because Liberty is unworkable, but because we have not worked it conscientiously or have forgotten its true meaning that we often get the notion of the irreconcilable conflict with the Machine Age.

GOVERNMENT DICTATION OF BUSINESS AND AGRICULTURE

We cannot extend mastery of government over the daily life of a people without somewhere making it master of people's souls and thoughts. That is going on today. It is part of all regimentation.

Even if the government conduct of business could give us the maximum of efficiency instead of least efficiency, it would be purchased at the cost of freedom. It would increase rather than decrease abuse and corruption, stifle initiative and invention, undermine the development of leadership, cripple the mental and spiritual energies of our people, extinguish equality of opportunity, and dry up the spirit of liberty and the forces which make progress.

It is a false Liberalism that interprets itself into government dictation, or operation of commerce, industry and agriculture. Every move in that direction poisons the very springs of true Liberalism. It poisons political equality, free thought, free press, and equality of opportunity. It is the road not to liberty but to less liberty. True Liberalism is found not in striving to spread bureaucracy, but in striving to set bounds to it. Liberalism is a force proceeding from the deep realization that economic freedom cannot be sacrificed if political freedom is to be preserved. True Liberalism seeks all legitimate freedom first in the confident belief that without such freedom the pursuit of other blessings is in vain.

PROCESSES OF PROGRESS

The nation seeks for solution of its many difficulties. These solutions can come alone through the constructive forces from the system built upon Liberty. They cannot be achieved by the destructive forces of Regimentation. The purification of Liberty from abuses, the restoration of confidence in the rights of men, the release of the dynamic forces of initiative and enterprise are alone the methods by which these solutions can be found and the purpose of American life assured.

The structure of human betterment cannot by built upon foundations of materialism or business, but upon the bedrock of individual character in free men and women. It must be builded by those who, holding to ideals of its high purpose, using the molds of justice, lay brick upon brick from the materials of scientific research, the painstaking sifting of truth from collections of facts and experience, the advancing ideas, morals and spiritual inspirations. Any other foundations are sand, any other mold is distorted; and any other bricks are without straw.

THE SPARK OF LIBERTY

I have no fear that the inherent and unconquerable forces of freedom will not triumph. But it is as true today as when first uttered that "the condition upon which God hath given liberty to man is eternal vigilance." We have in our lifetime seen the subjection of Liberty in one nation after another. It has been defeated by the untruth that some form of dictation by government alone can overcome immediate difficulties and can assure entry into economic perfection. America must not and it will not succumb to that lure. That is the issue of our generation, not a partisan issue but the issue of human liberty.

The spark of liberty in the mind and spirit of man cannot be long extinguished; it will break into flames that will destroy every coercion which seeks to limit it.